Cover Artist · Emily Fiegenschuh
Interior Artists · Donald Crank, Ian Llanas, Ian Perks,
    Fernanda Suarez, Andy Timm, Kuba Witowski,
    and Vicky Yarova

Creative Director · James Jacobs
Editor-in-Chief · F. Wesley Schneider
Managing Editor · James L. Sutter
Lead Developers · Patrick Renie and
    Owen K.C. Stephens

Senior Developer · Rob McCreary
Developers · John Compton, Adam Daigle,
    Mark Moreland, Patrick Renie, and
    Owen K.C. Stephens
Associate Editors · Judy Bauer and Christopher Carey
Editors · Joe Homes and Ryan Macklin
Lead Designer · Jason Bulmahn
Designers · Logan Bonner, Stephen Radney-MacFarland,
    and Mark Seifter

Managing Art Director · Sarah E. Robinson
Senior Art Director · Andrew Vallas
Art Director · Sonja Morris
Graphic Designers · Emily Crowell and Ben Mouch

Publisher · Erik Mona
Paizo CEO · Lisa Stevens
Chief Operations Officer · Jeffrey Alvarez
Director of Sales · Pierce Watters
Sales Associate · Cosmo Eisele
Marketing Director · Jenny Bendel
Finance Manager · Christopher Self
Staff Accountant · Ashley Kaprielian
Data Entry Clerk · B. Scott Keim
Chief Technical Officer · Vic Wertz
Software Development Manager · Cort Odekirk
Senior Software Developer · Gary Teter
Campaign Coordinator · Mike Brock
Project Manager · Jessica Price
Licensing Coordinator · Michael Kenway

Customer Service Team · Sharaya Kemp,
    Katina Mathieson, Sara Marie Teter, and Diego Valdez
Warehouse Team · Will Chase, Mika Hawkins,
    Heather Payne, Jeff Strand, and Kevin Underwood
Website Team · Christopher Anthony, Liz Courts,
    Winslow Dalpe, Lissa Guillet, Erik Keith, and
    Chris Lambertz

On the Cover

Seoni the sorcerer gets familiar with a crowd of animal aides and otherwordly helpers in this cover by Emily Fiegenschuh.

Table of Contents

Reference

This Pathfinder Player Companion refers to several other Pathfinder Roleplaying Game products and uses the following abbreviations. These books are not required to make use of this Player Companion. Readers interested in references to Pathfinder RPG hardcovers can find the complete rules from these books available for free at **paizo.com/prd**.

Advanced Player's Guide	APG	*Ultimate Combat*	UC

Paizo Inc.
7120 185th Ave NE, Ste 120
Redmond, WA 98052-0577

paizo.com

For Your Character

Focus Characters

This Pathfinder Player Companion highlights new options specific to characters of the following classes, as well as elements that can apply to a wide array of characters.

Bloodragers

Bloodragers gain access to a diverse range of familiars through the bloodline familiar rules. Coupled with the martial-themed familiar archetypes such as mauler and protector (page 11), this allows bloodragers to use familiars as effective assistants in combat.

Fighters

Though fighters gain only a single archetype, the eldritch guardian (page 7), its inclusion is significant because fighters do not normally have access to any form of familiar or animal companion. This allows fighters to take advantage of the many options in this volume.

Witches

As the only character class that has familiars as an integral part of its abilities rather than an optional feature, the witch benefits greatly from the options presented in this volume. The expanded list of familiars pages 24–31) gives players more selection when trying to match a familiar to a specific witch character concept. Patron familiars (page 17) have special ties to witches' patrons, further strengthening the bond between witch and familiar.

Wizards

These masters of magic have much to gain throughout this volume. The familiar adept, pact wizard, and spirit binder archetypes (pages 8–9) and school-specific familiars (pages 14–15) allow each wizard to customize his familiar to better support his specific selection of spells and combat tactics.

For Every Character

Certain game elements transcend the particulars of a character's race or class. The following elements detailed in this book work equally well for any character you want to play, allowing even adventurers without familiars new ways to interact with the familiars of others.

Approximating New Familiars

The guidelines for handling a player's request for a familiar that doesn't exist (pages 12–13) can also be used to expand players' choices of animal companions, cohorts, followers, and summoned creatures, making them potentially applicable by a wide range of adventurers.

Archetypes

In addition to options for the focus character classes, there are archetypes that make familiars a possibility for alchemists, bards, druids, magi, and paladins.

Favored Familiars

The information on the most common familiars among various cultures, groups, and nations (pages 5–6) can help develop characters associated with those groups, even if the character doesn't have a familiar. When playing a character who opposes the hellknights, it can be useful to know that signifers have a fondness for imp familiars—for planning purposes, if nothing else.

Gear and Magic Items

Much of the new equipment in this volume (pages 20–21) is designed to deal with the familiars of hostile spellcasters. The poison introduced

Questions to Ask Your GM

Asking your Game Master the following questions can help you get the most out of *Pathfinder Player Companion: Familiar Folio*.

1 Does my choice of familiar make sense for our campaign? Is there a sort of familiar especially appropriate for this campaign?

2 Is my character's familiar controlled by me—the player in charge of its master—or will it be controlled by the GM as an NPC?

3 Are familiars from other sources, such as the various *Bestiary* volumes, available for use in this campaign?

in this section can be useful for sowing dissent among any allies, and can even allow a character to be inured to the manipulations of charismatic foes.

New Improved Familiars

Though available as improved familiars, the new monsters introduced on pages 28–29 of this volume have high enough Intelligence scores that they could potentially be hired as mercenary spies or befriended to serve as willing allies.

Spells

Some of the new spells introduced on pages 22–23 are designed to boost an ally's familiar, or disable the familiar of a foe.

Teamwork Feats

New teamwork feats (page 18) allow spellcasters without familiars to take advantage of an ally's familiar.

DID YOU KNOW?

The original draft of the witch from the *Pathfinder RPG Advanced Player's Guide* included the goat and pig as potential familiars. Both of these were eventually cut during playtesting, but the ideas remained popular enough for them to reappear as options in *Pathfinder RPG Bestiary 3*.

Rules Index

The following new rules options are presented in this Pathfinder Player Companion.

Introduction

Throughout Golarion, familiars appear as the servants and comrades of a variety of spellcasters. Their origins and connections to their masters are as diverse and mysterious as any caster's eldritch powers, and these small but versatile creatures are widely regarded with both fascination and wariness. In the Pathfinder RPG, familiars have a well-defined role and a predictable set of powers. Generally the companions of wizards and witches (and sometimes sorcerers, alchemists, and magi), familiars might assist their masters, scout ahead, and carry their masters' spells to foes. But all of this hardly scratches the surface of a familiar's potential. The following pages present a myriad of ways to redefine familiars and evoke the mystery and otherworldliness of these strange, magnificent allies.

Familiars in Play

In addition to all the features for spellcasters in this book, some of the new options herein give non-spellcasters the chance to gain their own familiars. While the role of the spell-delivering avian or the serpentine spy has been well defined by countless characters with familiar allies, there's endless potential for familiars to assist other classes. Whether you're a cunning trickster using your pets as a magical co-conspirator or a warrior using clever tactics with your ferocious animals having a wily and easily underestimated ally can help you with more than just spellcasting.

Aside from their benefits on the battlefield, familiars also provide unique opportunities for players to roleplay creatures quite different from their usual characters. Check with your GM to see how she plans to incorporate the familiar into the game; ask whether she plans to roleplay the familiar's personality, or if the familiar is yours to control. If the latter is the case, you might want to make your familiar more than just another character ability. Think about the creature's character and, as it progresses, its evolving personality. Perhaps your familiar is a crow that collects trinkets from gravesites or an irritable viper that startles easily. While you don't want your familiar to upstage your character, it can be so much more than a collection of numbers.

Familiars can also significantly complement their masters, whether in style, connection to backstories, or otherwise. The wisdom suggested by an owl rubs off on its spellcaster master, in the same way that a fiendish familiar might suggest an insidious pact. A character might come from a line of spellcasters known for their connection to eagles or who have shared the same otherworldly ally. Consider what your familiar might mean to your character and how it might reflect upon him or her in play.

There are dozens of different familiars to choose from. Check out the inside front and back covers for a full list of familiars and improved familiars, then choose which best fits your character!

Favored Familiars

Different cultures and organizations value different types of familiars, depending on their principles and activities. Presented here is a list of significant Inner Sea organizations and the kinds of familiars their members favor.

Acadamae: The Acadamae takes its traditions from infernal Cheliax, so summoning imps is common—to the point where the city of Korvosa is riddled with imps and the pseudodragons that hunt them. School familiars (see page 14), particularly of the conjuration and enchantment schools, prove quite common.

Arclords: The Arclords of Nex appreciate familiars that show off their masters' ingenuity and innovation, so they often favor exotic creatures such as archaeopteryxes, rhamphorhynchuses, and tuataras. Homuncului are also a favorite choice, as they embody the creative will of their masters. Since the Arcanamirium in Absalom was founded by the Arclords, it scholars share these biases in part, but tend to have more varied preferences.

Aspis Consortium: Aspis agents often prefer familiars that can aid them in their various semi-legal ventures. Animals that can easily infiltrate buildings or filch goods number among their favorites, particularly those with hands to quietly open doors and chests, such as monkeys, mephits, and many other improved familiars.

Blackfire Adepts: Blackfire adepts seek familiars who embody the wildness of the planes. Their favorite familiars include chaotic and evil outsiders like cacodaemons, imps, quasits, and voidworms.

Blood Lords: The rulers of Geb desire companions that can last as long as they do, such as undead, constructs, and outsiders that are effectively immortal. When they select animals, the Blood Lords prefer those with a connection to death, notably ravens and vultures.

Esoteric Order of the Palatine Eye: These students of the occult favor familiars that compliment their study of the forbidden and forgotten. Cats, bats, toads, and greensting scorpions are favorites. Pseudosphinxes and psychopomps also tie into many members' interest in the history of Osirion.

Hellknights: Hellknight signifers with familiars value loyalty and discipline above all. They favor social animals that understand hierarchies and prove useful in battle, like dogs and hawks. Hellknights are also fond of familiars that embody the rigidity of law, like arbiters and imps.

Magaambyan Arcanists: Magaambyan arcanists often choose creatures with gentle, tranquil, or elusive natures—like bats and weasels—as well as creatures local to the Mwangi Expanse like monkeys and dinosaurs. The druidic bent of this organization makes it easy for members to bond with fey such as sprites and brownies.

Pathfinder Society: Pathfinder Society field agents employ familiars as diverse as the agents themselves. In keeping with the Society's tenets, the only familiars that are less common among agents are evil outsiders, since such beings often have their own malignant agendas and can place their masters at odds with their comrades.

FAMILIAR TACTICS

Using familiars as scouts and having them deliver touch spells are standard practices for adventurers willing to put their allies at risk of attack. Here are several more ideas for tactics you might coordinate with your familiar.

Device Guru: If you have enough ranks in Use Magic Device or choose magic items that don't require such checks, your familiar can activate a wide variety of magic items for you. As long as the familiar can speak (like most improved familiars and a few birds) and hold or wear the item as necessary, it can activate command word items and attempt the necessary check to activate a wand, scroll, or staff. Faerie dragons (who can activate wands without a skill check), lyrakien (who have high Charisma scores), and pookas (who gain Use Magic Device as a class skill) are all excellent choices.

Logistical Helper: Sometimes a great plan requires more actions than are available to the PCs. Perhaps the cleric wants to use a *scroll of breath of life* to save the fighter, but she can't draw the scroll, advance, and read it all on the same turn. Sometimes you run out of hands and have to drop something, only to need it again later in the fight. Why not have a familiar help out? The familiar can act as a convenient retriever of any items it can carry. If nothing else, the familiar can use the aid another action on skill checks (it has all your ranks, after all), and even in fights to bolster the party's offense or defense. This is particularly useful with improved familiars that can hold reach weapons and flank with you!

Mini Mage: Though rare, there are a few spells with a range of personal that allow a familiar to serve an interesting combat role. For instance, *burning gaze* (*Pathfinder RPG Advanced Player's Guide* 208) allows a familiar to become a minor evoker, and *elemental aura* (*Advanced Player's Guide* 218) enables a familiar to deal damage as it moves around a battlefield.

Prophets of Kalistrade: The covetous followers of the Prophecies of Kalistrade often view familiars as status symbols—the rarer and more impressive, the better. Creatures like parrots, peacocks, and breeds of colorful snakes and lizards prove particularly popular, and the prophets regularly buy rich accessories to even further accent their allies. Pampered carbuncles also hold a special place in the homes and entourages of several prophets.

Riftwardens: The Riftwardens' primary concern is the integrity of the Great Beyond, so they tend to choose familiars that are native to the planes to which they feel the greatest connection. On Golarion, these might be ordinary animals like cats, dogs, and rabbits.

Winter Witches: Irrisen's infamous mistresses of cold prefer creatures that can endure their homeland's arctic climes such as foxes, hares, and penguins. Improved familiars with affinities for ice, such as ice mephits and ice elementals, are also favored.

Character Archetypes

The following archetypes grant familiars to classes that normally do not have access to them.

Chosen One (Paladin Archetype)

Most paladins train for years at a temple to attain a holy status, but rarely, an emissary of the divine appears to one of humble origins and calls her directly to the charge. These chosen ones may lack experience, but their teamwork with their emissaries allows them to defeat any evil.

Bondless: A chosen one does not gain the divine bond class feature.

Divine Emissary (Ex): At 1st level, a chosen one gains an emissary familiar (see page 10), treating her paladin level as her wizard level for the purpose of this ability.

Religious Mentor (Ex): The familiar's sworn duty is to help train the chosen one for her future glory. The familiar is treated as having a number of ranks in Knowledge (religion) equal to the chosen one's paladin level. The chosen one doesn't gain Knowledge (religion) as a class skill.

Delayed Grace (Su): A chosen one begins her adventuring career without fully understanding her true potential. The chosen one uses the Barbarian, Rogue, Sorcerer column on Table 7–1 on page 169 of the *Pathfinder RPG Core Rulebook* to calculate her typical starting age. She receives the smite evil ability at 2nd level and the divine grace ability at 4th level. This does not affect the rate at which she gains additional uses per day of smite evil, so she still gains her second use at 4th level, her third at 7th level, and so on. This ability alters divine grace and smite evil.

Lay on Paws (Su): At 2nd level, a chosen one's familiar is able to borrow some of her divine energy to heal itself and others. The familiar can use the chosen one's lay on hands ability, including all of her mercies, but each such use consumes two uses of the paladin's lay on hands ability. Starting at 4th level, the familiar can also channel positive energy, but each such use consumes four uses of the paladin's lay on hands ability. This ability alters lay on hands and channel positive energy.

True Form (Ex): At 7th level, a chosen one's familiar reveals its true form, transforming into an outsider improved familiar that matches the chosen one's patron's alignment (typically an arbiter, a cassisian, a harbinger, or a silvanshee, but potentially any lawful neutral, lawful good, or neutral good outsider familiar depending on the patron). The familiar gains the change shape universal monster ability if it doesn't already have it, which it can use at will to transform into its original form or back to its true form.

Emissary's Smite (Su): At 11th level, a chosen one's familiar also benefits from the paladin's smite evil ability whenever the chosen one uses smite evil.

Duettist (Bard Archetype)

Whether singing a delicate duo with a nightingale or slipping coins from purses while a trained monkey distracts the crowd, the duettist blends his bond to his familiar with his natural talent for performance to create amazing effects.

Diminished Competency: A duettist does not gain the well-versed or jack-of-all-trades class features.

Familiar (Ex): At 1st level, a duettist gains a familiar, treating his bard level as his effective wizard level for the purpose of this ability. This ability replaces bardic knowledge.

Versatile Familiar (Ex): At 2nd level, a duettist's familiar learns to use performance to supplement its skills. A duettist's familiar benefits from its master's versatile performance class feature. This ability alters versatile performance.

Performing Familiar (Su): At 4th level, a duettist's familiar learns how to create supernatural effects with its performances, just like its master. The familiar can use any of its master's bardic performances, but only the familiar or the duettist can have a performance active at any given time, not both. If one is performing and the other starts a performance, the previous performance immediately ends. Each round that the familiar performs consumes 2 rounds of the duettist's bardic performance. This ability replaces lore master.

Harmonizing Familiar (Su): At 8th level, the duettist and his familiar have learned how to perform together in harmony. When a duettist and his familiar perform the same bardic performance simultaneously, its effects are enhanced. If the performance has a DC, the DC increases by 2. If the performance provides a competence bonus, the competence bonus increases by 1. Because both the duettist and the familiar are performing, each round performed consumes 3 rounds of bardic performance. This ability replaces dirge of doom.

Symphonic Familiar (Su): At 14th level, the duettist and his familiar have learned how to create a symphony of complementary performances that meld together to produce two different effects. They can each perform a different bardic performance simultaneously, and each has its full effect. Because both the duettist and the familiar are performing, each round performed consumes 3 rounds of bardic performance. This ability replaces frightening tune.

Eldritch Guardian (Fighter Archetype)

Eldritch guardians are trained to detect and give warning about magic threats to the people and places they protect.

Class Skills: The eldritch guardian adds Perception, Spellcraft, and Use Magic Device to his list of class skills, but does not gain Intimidate, Ride, or Swim as class skills.

Familiar (Ex): At 1st level, an eldritch guardian gains a familiar, treating his fighter level as his effective wizard level for the purpose of this ability. This ability replaces the bonus feat gained at 1st level.

Share Training (Ex): At 2nd level, when the familiar can see and hear its master, it can use any combat feat possessed by the eldritch guardian. The familiar doesn't have to meet the feat's prerequisites, but at the GM's discretion may be precluded from using certain combat feats due to its physical form. For example, an eldritch guardian's pig familiar with access to Exotic Weapon Proficiency (spiked chain) would not gain the ability to use spiked chains, since it doesn't have any limbs capable of properly handling them. This ability replaces the bonus feat gained at 2nd level.

Steel Will (Ex): At 2nd level, the eldritch guardian gains a +1 bonus on Will saves against fear and mind-affecting effects. This bonus increases by 1 for every 4 levels beyond 2nd. This ability replaces bravery.

Leshy Warden (Druid Archetype)

The natural world is full of bodiless nature spirits connected to the forces of springs, glades, and individual plants. Some druids hear their call keenly and are able to effortlessly incarnate them as the miniature creatures known as leshies (*Pathfinder RPG Bestiary 3* 176). The leshy warden serves as these spirits' voice, defender, and ally.

Leshy Familiar (Ex): At 1st level, a leshy warden forms an intimate bond with a nature spirit, incarnating the spirit as a leaf leshy (see the Unusual Familiars sidebar on page 31). She gains a leaf leshy as a familiar and treats her druid level as her effective wizard level for the purpose of this ability. If the leshy dies, the leshy warden can incarnate the same spirit again by paying the normal cost to replace a familiar. So long as the leshy lives, the leshy warden gains access to the Plant domain as if through a druid's nature bond class feature, but she can't choose the Decay subdomain. This ability replaces nature bond.

Green Empathy (Ex): At 1st level, a leshy warden can improve the attitude of a plant creature as if using wild empathy. The typical wild plant creature has a starting attitude of indifferent. A leshy warden can also use this ability to influence an animal, but she takes a –4 penalty on the check to do so. This ability replaces wild empathy.

Leshy Caller (Ex): A leshy warden is an expert at summoning and growing leshies. She counts as a plant creature for the purpose of growing leshies. She adds leaf leshies, gourd leshies, fungus leshies, and seaweed leshies to her list of creatures for *summon nature's ally I, II, III,* and *IV*, respectively.

Leshy Tender (Ex): At 4th level, a leshy warden chooses either to grant her leaf leshy a +2 increase to Strength and Dexterity or to transform it into a gourd leshy. At 8th level, the leshy warden can either grant her current leshy a +2 increase to Strength and Dexterity or transform it into a fungus leshy. Finally, at 12th level, she can either grant her current leshy a final +2 increase to Strength and Dexterity or transform it into a seaweed leshy. If the leshy is transformed, it gains the normal ability scores of its new form—the ability score increases granted by this ability don't carry over to its new form.

Wild Shape (Su): A leshy warden gains this ability at 6th level, except her effective druid level for the ability is equal to her druid level – 2 for the purpose of determining the number of times per day she may use it. At 6th level, the leshy warden can assume the form of only Small or Medium plant creatures, as *plant shape I*. At 8th level, she can take the form of a Large plant creature, as *plant shape II*. At 10th level, she can take the form of a Huge plant creature, as *plant shape III*.

Spirit Whisperer (Su): At 13th level, a leshy warden's connection to the spirits of nature becomes strong enough that she can always hear them whispering. She is treated as constantly under the effects of *speak with plants*. Once per day, she can spend 10 minutes in communion with the spirits to learn the answers to her questions, as *commune with nature*. This ability replaces a thousand faces.

Caster Archetypes

The following new class archetypes modify classes that already have access to familiars, with a focus on making the familiar an essential aspect of the class's abilities.

Beastblade (Magus Archetype)

Beastblade magi work in tandem with their familiars, using spell, steel, and claw to clear the battlefield of foes.

Familiar (Ex): At 3rd level, the beastblade gains the familiar magus arcana. This ability replaces the magus arcana gained at 3rd level.

Tandem Touch (Su): At 4th level, while the beastblade's familiar is holding the charge for a touch spell, the beastblade can cast another spell without discharging the familiar's held charge. This ability replaces spell recall.

Familiar Pool (Su): At 7th level, when a beastblade prepares his magus spells, he can expend points from his arcane pool (up to a maximum number of points equal to his Intelligence modifier) to empower his familiar. For each point expended in this way, the familiar can cast one magus spell as a spell-like ability once that day. Each spell selected must be 3 spell levels lower than the highest spell level the beastblade can cast, and can't require a material component that costs more than 1 gp. This ability replaces knowledge pool.

Familiar Spellstrike (Su): At 11th level, whenever a beastblade's familiar successfully delivers a touch spell against a creature the magus threatens, the target provokes an attack of opportunity from the magus. This ability replaces improved spell recall.

Familiar Adept (Wizard Archetype)

Many wizards employ familiars to assist them, but only a few have unlocked the true power of their school of magic through the familiar itself.

Diminished Expertise: A familiar adept doesn't gain Scribe Scroll at 1st level or the wizard's bonus feats at 5th and 10th levels. He must also choose one additional opposition school, even if he is a universalist.

School Familiar (Ex): At 1st level, a familiar adept must select a familiar for his arcane bond. His familiar automatically gains the school familiar archetype (see page 14), but it cannot use its lesser school power until 4th level. At 8th level, it gains access to its greater school power. This ability alters arcane bond.

Familiar Spells (Ex): A familiar adept stores his spells in his familiar rather than in a spellbook, exactly as a witch does. His familiar can freely trade spells known with a witch's familiar, provided the spells traded are on both casters' class spell lists. The familiar adept's familiar uses the witch rules for familiars, including the increased cost of replacing the familiar. This ability alters spellbooks.

Focused School (Ex): A familiar adept's training is focused more deeply on his familiar and his school of magic. At 1st level, 5th level, and every 5 levels thereafter, his familiar gains the ability to use the wizard's 1st-level school ability one time per day without it counting against the wizard's daily uses.

Homunculist (Alchemist Archetype)

One of the grand goals of alchemy is the ability to create new life. A homunculist has made this dream a reality, growing and modifying a familiar in his own laboratory.

Diminished Poisoning: A homunculist doesn't gain the poison use, poison resistance, poison immunity, or swift poisoning class features.

Homunculus Familiar (Ex): The homunculist has created a living homunculus (*Pathfinder RPG Bestiary* 176) in the shape of an animal or vermin. It functions in all ways as a familiar, treating the homunculist's alchemist level as his effective wizard level. This ability replaces mutagen.

Experimentation (Ex): A homunculist is constantly experimenting on his familiar to give it new and unusual features and abilities. At 4th level, the homunculist can grant his familiar 1 evolution point worth of eidolon evolutions (*Pathfinder RPG Advanced Player's Guide* 60) for every 4 alchemist levels he possesses, though he can't select any evolutions that require a particular base form. Each time the homunculist gains a level, he can change his familiar's evolutions. These evolutions stack with those from the Evolved Familiar feat (*Pathfinder RPG Ultimate Magic* 149). The homunculist can select the Evolved Familiar feat as an alchemist discovery if he meets its prerequisites.

Pact Wizard (Wizard Archetype)

Some wizards make bargains with beings from other realms in order to gain arcane power. These pact wizards have unparalleled access to extraplanar allies, but these bonds never come without strings attached.

Familiar (Ex): A pact wizard must select a familiar for his arcane bond. The familiar's loyalty ultimately lies with the pact wizard's patron, and it reports back to the patron on the wizard's activities. This ability alters arcane bond.

Pact Focus (Ex): At 1st level, a pact wizard must choose one additional opposition school, even if he is a universalist. A pact wizard can't pick conjuration as an opposition school. This ability alters arcane school.

Pact (Ex): A pact wizard enters into a bargain with an extraplanar being in order to gain increased wizardly powers. At 1st level, he selects a patron belonging to one specific subtype of outsider for which there exists an improved familiar option (such as devil or azata). The pact wizard can select a subtype of outsider even with a diametrically opposed alignment; in this case, the patron being offers the pact in an attempt to tempt or redeem the pact wizard. A pact wizard whose alignment shifts away from the chosen outsider subtype, who grossly abuses his familiar or any outsider of the chosen subtype, or who commits egregious acts against the alignment of the patron loses all the benefits of this archetype (but keeps the additional opposition school) until he receives an *atonement*.

Aura (Ex): A pact wizard has an aura corresponding to the alignment of his chosen subtype as a cleric of his wizard level.

Pact Summons (Ex): A pact wizard can select Sacred Summons (*Pathfinder RPG Ultimate Magic* 155) as a wizard bonus feat. He can use this feat only to summon outsiders of his chosen subtype.

True Form (Ex): At 7th level, a pact wizard's familiar reveals its true form, automatically transforming into an outsider improved familiar of the chosen subtype.

Spirit Binder (Wizard Archetype)

While most wizards learn their arts through gradual study, spirit binders have made a sudden arcane breakthrough due to the traumatic experience of losing a loved one.

Soulbound Familiar (Ex): A spirit binder must select a familiar for his arcane bond. Unlike in a normal familiar-summoning ritual, a spirit binder created his special familiar through a dangerous ritual catalyzed by the death of a loved one. Before the loved one's spirit passed on to the Boneyard, the spirit binder was able to bind the spirit to an animal or vermin, which then became his familiar.

A soulbound familiar's personality is that of the lost loved one, rather than a servant of the spirit binder. It can have any alignment, even one that is diametrically opposed to the spirit binder's. A soulbound familiar has the base attack bonus and base saving throws of the loved one's favored class (using the spirit binder's level as its level). If the loved one died before the beginning of the campaign, the spirit binder selects the familiar's favored class at 1st level and it cannot be changed. This ability alters arcane bond.

Arcane School: A spirit binder can't choose necromancy as an opposition school. This ability alters arcane school.

Lost Talents (Ex): A spirit binder's soulbound familiar possesses some of the ability of the lost loved one, and it is capable of learning more. At 1st level, 5th level, and every 5 levels thereafter, the spirit binder's familiar gains a new feat for which it meets the prerequisites. This ability replaces Scribe Scroll and the wizard's bonus feats.

Synergist (Witch Archetype)

Synergists gain the ability to combine their forms with their familiars' in order to create something more powerful than either alone.

Symbiosis (Su): At 1st level, a synergist gains the ability to meld or unmeld with her familiar as a standard action. While the familiar is melded, its body becomes part of the synergist's and can't be targeted or affected by any means (including ongoing effects), though the familiar can still communicate its feelings empathically. The symbiosis causes the synergist to adopt some basic physical features of the familiar and grants additional abilities based on the synergist's level.

At 1st level, during symbiosis the synergist gains darkvision or low-light vision if the familiar possesses it.

At 5th level, during symbiosis the synergist gains any abilities the familiar possesses that are listed under *beast shape I*, except flight.

At 8th level, during symbiosis the synergist gains any abilities the familiar possesses that are listed under *beast shape II*. If the familiar can fly, the synergist can fly for a total of 1 minute per witch level she possesses per day while in symbiosis. This duration need not be consecutive, but it must be spent in 1-minute intervals.

Additionally, during symbiosis the synergist gains a single natural attack of a type possessed by its familiar. The attack deals 1d6 points of damage if a primary attack (1d6 for Small synergists) and 1d4 points of damage if a secondary attack (1d3 for Small synergists).

At 11th level, during symbiosis the synergist gains any abilities the familiar possesses that are listed under *beast shape III*. If the familiar can fly, the synergist can fly for an unlimited amount of time each day while in symbiosis.

At 14th level, during symbiosis the synergist gains any abilities the familiar possesses that are listed under *beast shape IV*. If the familiar has multiple natural attacks, the synergist gains them all, rather than just one.

This ability replaces the hexes gained at 1st, 8th, and 14th level.

Familiar Archetypes

Familiar archetypes modify familiars' standard abilities, similar to how class archetypes modify player characters' class features. These archetypes function by swapping out certain abilities that are standard to common familiars for new abilities tailored to particular themes.

Unless otherwise stated, levels referenced in this section refer to the familiar's effective level, which is the master's combined levels in the classes that grant that familiar.

Decoy (Familiar Archetype)

A decoy misdirects its master's enemies, allowing the master to strike by surprise.

Class Skills: A decoy treats Bluff as a class skill.

Deceitful: A decoy gains Deceitful as a bonus feat. This replaces alertness.

Mockingbird (Ex): At 5th level, a decoy can speak any of its master's languages. At 7th level, it can mimic its master's voice and intonation perfectly. This ability replaces speak with master and speak with animals of its kind.

Master's Guise (Sp): At 11th level, a decoy can transform into a perfect likeness of its master, as the *alter self* spell. It can hold this form for up to 1 minute per caster level; upon changing back, the decoy must remain in its natural form

for an equal amount of time before transforming again. This ability replaces spell resistance.

Emissary (Familiar Archetype)

The emissary is touched by the divine, serving as a font of wisdom and a moral compass for its master.

Class Skills: An emissary treats Heal, Knowledge (religion), and Sense Motive as class skills.

Divine Guidance (Sp): An emissary can cast *guidance* at will. This ability replaces alertness.

Share Will (Su): Whenever an emissary or its master fails a save against a mind-affecting effect that affects only one of them, the other can choose to attempt the save as well. If this second save succeeds, treat the original save result as a success, and the emissary and its master can't use this ability again for 24 hours. On a failure, both the emissary and its master suffer the effects of the failed saving throw, even if one of them wouldn't ordinarily be a valid target. This ability replaces share spells.

Domain Influence (Sp or Su): At 3rd level, the emissary gains a spark of divine power from the patron that sent it. Choose one appropriate domain that grants a 1st-level domain power usable a number of times per day equal to 3 + the user's Wisdom modifier. The emissary can use that power once per day. This ability replaces deliver touch spells.

Figment (Familiar Archetype)

Figments are born from their masters' imaginations rather than awakened from ordinary creatures.

Recurring Dream (Su): A figment has a total number of hit points equal to 1/4 the master's total hit points. If the figment dies, it vanishes, appearing again with 1 hit point after its master awakens from a full night's sleep. If a figment ever strays more than 100 feet from its master, a figment enters an *antimagic field*, or a figment's master is rendered unconscious or asleep, the figment disappears until the next time its master prepares spells or regains spells per day. Because it is a being of its master's own mind, a figment can never serve as a witch's familiar, and

it can't use any divination spells or spell-like abilities it may possess. This ability replaces improved evasion.

Manifest Dreams (Su): At 3rd level, a figment is shaped by its master's dreams. Each time the master awakens from a full night's rest, he can apply to the figment 1 evolution point worth of eidolon evolutions that don't have a base form requirement. At 7th level, he can apply 2 points worth of evolutions; at 13th level, he can apply 3 points worth of eidolon evolutions. This ability replaces deliver touch spells, speak with animals of its kind, and scry on familiar.

Mascot (Familiar Archetype)

A familiar sometimes serves as the centerpiece of an adventuring party, eventually binding the team together into a collective master.

Class Skills: A mascot treats all Perform skills as class skills.

Affinity for My Team (Su): A mascot is the heart and soul of its team, which at first consists of only the familiar and its master. At 1st level and every 3 levels thereafter, a mascot can add an additional member to its team. A mascot's empathic link extends to all members of its team. A mascot can add or remove one team member over the course of a day. If a team member dies, the mascot gains 1 permanent negative level. This ability replaces alertness and alters empathic link.

Lucky Mascot (Su): Whenever a mascot uses the aid another action to aid a team member's attack roll or AC, that team member also gains a +1 luck bonus on all attack rolls or to AC for 1 round. This ability replaces improved evasion.

Share Spells: At 3rd level, spells targeting a mascot via its share spells ability function at its level − 2. The mascot can benefit from the spells of any team member when using share spells.

Deliver Touch Spells (Su): At 5th level, spells delivered by a mascot's deliver touch spells ability function at its level − 2. The mascot can deliver the touch spells of any team member. This ability alters deliver touch spells.

Speak with Team (Ex): At 7th level, a mascot gains the ability to speak with all members of its team verbally as if using speak with master. This ability replaces speak with master and speak with animals of its kind.

Heart of the Team (Ex): At 13th level, as a full-round action, a mascot can designate any member of its team as its master for the purposes of calculating its Hit Dice, hit points, base attack bonus, saving throws, and skill ranks. This ability replaces spell resistance and scry on familiar.

Mauler (Familiar Archetype)

While most familiars are scouts and assistants, the mauler familiar cares only for the thrill of battle. A mauler often serves a bloodthirsty or martial-minded master.

Class Skills: A mauler treats Intimidate as a class skill.

Bond Forged in Blood (Su): A mauler isn't impressed by fancy words—only furious battle. A mauler can't speak, even if it's a type of creature that normally could.

At 5th level, whenever the mauler's master drops a foe whose Hit Dice are at least 1/2 its level to below 0 hit points, the mauler's empathic link surges with power, granting both the mauler and its master a +2 morale bonus to attack and damage rolls for 1 round. This ability replaces speak with master and speak with animals of its kind.

Increased Strength (Ex): At 3rd level and every 2 levels thereafter, a mauler's Strength score increases by 1. As a result of this ability, the familiar's Intelligence score remains 6; a mauler can never have an Intelligence score higher than 6.

Battle Form (Su): At 3rd level, a mauler gains the ability to transform into a larger, more ferocious form and back at will. In battle form, the mauler's size becomes Medium and the mauler gains a +2 bonus to Strength (this stacks with the normal Strength adjustments for increasing in size). This ability replaces deliver touch spells.

Damage Reduction (Su): At 11th level, a mauler gains DR 5/magic. This ability replaces spell resistance.

Protector (Familiar Archetype)

Protector familiars are so devoted that they would gladly give their lives for their masters.

Loyal Bodyguard (Ex): A protector gains Bodyguard (*Pathfinder RPG Advanced Player's Guide* 151) and Combat Reflexes as bonus feats. If the familiar is occupying its master's square, it can use Bodyguard to aid another to improve its master's AC even if it doesn't threaten the attacking foe. This ability replaces alertness and improved evasion.

Shield Master (Su): At 5th level, whenever a protector or its master takes hit point damage, as long as the protector and its master are touching, its master can choose to split the damage evenly between them as if using *shield other*. This ability replaces deliver touch spells and speak with animals of its kind.

In Harm's Way: At 11th level, a protector gains In Harm's Way (*Advanced Player's Guide* 164) as a bonus feat. This ability replaces spell resistance.

Sage (Familiar Archetype)

Sage familiars are masters of useful facts, able to recall them for their master's benefit, though this leads many to become haughty and proud.

Class Skills: A sage treats all Knowledge skills as class skills.

Dazzling Intellect (Ex): A sage's Intelligence score is always equal to 5 + its level, but the sage gains the additional natural armor increases of a familiar only half its level. This ability alters the familiar's Intelligence score and natural armor adjustment.

Sage's Knowledge (Ex): A sage stores information on every topic and is happy to lecture its master on the finer points. A sage can attempt all Knowledge checks untrained and receives a bonus on all Knowledge checks equal to 1/2 its level. Additionally, a sage gains 2 skill ranks at each level. Its maximum number of ranks in any given skill is equal to its level. This ability replaces alertness and the familiar's ability to share its master's skill ranks.

Approximating Familiars

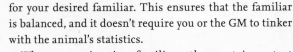

While there are already many kinds of familiars, sometimes the available options don't quite fit your vision of your character's magical companion. With your Game Master's approval, though, the statistics of an existing familiar can be repurposed to approximate the perfect familiar for your character.

Simple Method

The easiest way to formulate a familiar when there aren't already stats for the creature you're looking for is to examine the list on the inside front cover and find the animal closest to the one you have in mind. You can then simply use the statistics of the existing animal as those

for your desired familiar. This ensures that the familiar is balanced, and it doesn't require you or the GM to tinker with the animal's statistics.

When approximating familiars, the most important thing to realize is that a given familiar's statistics can be used to represent a wide variety of other creatures of the same creature type, not just that species. For example, the rat is a small, agile mammal, so it's a reasonable leap to use its statistics to represent a mouse, shrew, or other similar small mammal. Conversely, using the stats for a bat to represent a flying fish, despite some similarities, is probably suboptimal. Consider some of the Advanced Method options for making more significant adjustments to a creature.

The Approximate Familiars chart on the following page provides a list of the animal familiars most suitable for approximating other types of creatures, suggestions on what those creatures might be, and the sources of the statistics for the base animals. The suggestions listed beside each entry are not exhaustive, of course; they are merely there as guidelines to help you devise the perfect familiar for your character.

Advanced Method

You may want a familiar that is radically different from any other creature on the list. In these cases, your best bet is to select the familiar creature that is closest to what you're looking for, then work with your GM to come up with suitable ability substitutions or statistical alterations that bring the statistics in line with your imagined familiar. (Remember, always ask for your GM's approval before altering creature statistics or using homebrew elements in the game!)

You'll need to be well versed in the rules found in the appendices of the *Pathfinder RPG Bestiary* to create a balanced creature, and even if you do the math perfectly, your GM may still decide the creature is too powerful. Generally, the less dramatic the change to your familiar's base creature, the more balanced the resulting familiar will be. Players should always have a concrete theme in mind before adjusting familiars' statistics, preferably a concept that aims toward creating a familiar of an existing type that has a slightly specialized skill set. Creatures that are unique, though still largely natural, and tie into a character's backstory can also make good concepts.

Players who are considering altering a preexisting familiar should consider one or more of the following changes to the familiar's statistics, which are ordered from least to most impactful to the game mechanics.

Skills: Reverse-calculating where skill ranks went is generally easier with familiars than with other creatures, since familiars rarely have more than 1 Hit Die, and rarely have more than 1 or 2 skill ranks to begin with. Reallocating skill ranks can be an easy way of customizing a creature's statistics to better fit your image of your familiar's personality. For instance, to create a primate familiar that is good at stealing small trinkets, you might start with the statistics of a monkey and simply reallocate its skill ranks from Perception to Sleight of Hand or Stealth.

Feats: You can easily exchange a prebuilt familiar's starting feats with different feats that better match your concept, such as the familiar feats on page 18 of *Pathfinder Player Companion: Animal Archive*. There are also new feats relating to familiars on pages 18–19 of this volume, allowing a great deal of customization and sometimes adding unusual mystical qualities and abilities.

Attacks: While changing the damage dice for a creature's attacks can quickly create an underwhelming or overpowered familiar, exchanging natural attacks for other types of natural attacks is generally a safe practice. Using Table 3–1 from page 302 of the *Bestiary*, you can

easily switch out a bat's bite attack for two claws or a gore attack. Generally, you should replace a primary natural attack with another primary natural attack, and secondary attacks with other secondary attacks.

Speed: Changing a creature's movement types or speeds is usually to be avoided. However, it can be relatively safe as long as you are exchanging an unusual movement speed (such as a 10-foot burrow speed) for a different unusual movement speed of an equal rate (such as a 10-foot climb speed), or you are drastically reducing the creature's base land speed to give it an unusual movement speed (such as reducing a creature's 40-foot base land speed to 10 feet and granting the creature a 30-foot swim speed).

Ability Scores: Altering a creature's ability scores is the surest way to accidentally create an unbalanced creature, and isn't recommended for approximating new familiars in this manner.

Approximate Familiars

Base Familiar	Suggestions	Source
Archaeopteryx	Gliding possum, jeholornis, other primitive birds	*Bestiary 4* 96
Armadillo	Pampatheriidae, pangolin, pink fairy armadillo	*Animal Archive* 30
Bat	Anurognathus, finch, jeholopterus, onychonycteris	*Bestiary* 131
Cat	Lynx, Tasmanian devil	*Bestiary* 131
Blue-ringed octopus	Squid, octopus, other cephalopods	*Ultimate Magic* 117
Dinosaur, compsognathus	Erpetosuchus, water moccasin snake, other tiny venomous dinosaurs	*Bestiary 2* 90
Dodo	Bush moa, great auk	*Bestiary 4* 96
Donkey rat	Aardvark, anteater, beaver, capybara	*Ultimate Magic* 117
Fox	Coyote, dingo, prairie dog, tiny dog	*Bestiary 3* 112
Flying squirrel	Gliding possum, sugar glider	*Bestiary 3* 112
Goat	Deer, pudu, vampire deer	*Bestiary 3* 112
Greensting scorpion	Emperor scorpion, oversized insects	*Ultimate Magic* 118
Hawk	Eagle, osprey, peregrine falcon, snail kite	*Bestiary* 131
Hedgehog	Porcupine, tenrec	*Ultimate Magic* 119
House centipede	Millipede, scarab beetle, other venomous insects	*Ultimate Magic* 119
King crab	Crawfish, lobster, other crustaceans	*Ultimate Magic* 119
Leopard slug	Worm	See page 30
Lizard	Galago, salamander, slow loris	*Bestiary* 131
Monkey	Chimpanzee, lemur, tarsier, other tree-climbing primates	*Bestiary* 132
Otter	Beaver, grison, muskrat	*Bestiary 3* 113
Owl	Grouse, nighthawk, other nocturnal birds of prey	*Bestiary* 132
Pig	Peccary, tapir	*Bestiary 3* 113
Rabbit	Hare, jerboa, viscacha	*Animal Archive* 31
Raccoon	Circus monkey, coati, possum, red panda, sun bear	*Bestiary 3* 113
Rat	Guinea pig, mouse, shrew	*Bestiary* 132
Raven	Parakeet*, parrot*, toucan*	*Bestiary* 133
Scarlet spider	Cupboard spider, yellow sac spider, oversized insects	*Ultimate Magic* 120
Skunk	Striped polecat	*Bestiary 3* 247
Squirrel	Chinchilla, chipmunk, hamster	*Animal Archive* 31
Tuatara	Asian water dragon, dwarf caiman	*Bestiary 4* 97
Thrush	Bluebird, cardinal, sparrow, other diminutive birds	*Ultimate Magic* 120
Toad	Frog, xenopus, other amphibians	*Bestiary* 133
Turtle	Ostracoderm, tortoise	*Ultimate Magic* 120
Viper	Sea krait	*Bestiary* 133
Weasel	Ermine, ferret, mink, mongoose, stoat	*Bestiary* 133

* These suggestions don't receive the raven familiar's supernatural ability to speak a language.

School Familiars

A wizard who specializes in a specific school of magic and chooses a familiar for his arcane bond may benefit from a school-specific familiar—a magical beast with additional powers based on its master's arcane school.

Feats

The following feats enable characters with an arcane school to gain school-specific familiars.

School Familiar

Your familiar is tied to your school specialization.

Prerequisites: Familiar effective level 5th, specialized arcane school class feature.

Benefit: You can apply the school familiar archetype to your familiar.

Greater School Familiar

Your school familiar's powers are greater than others of its kind.

Prerequisites: School Familiar, wizard level 10th, specialized arcane school class feature.

Benefit: Your school familiar gains the greater school power from the school familiar archetype.

School Familiar (Familiar Archetype)

School familiars are tightly bound to the power of their master's chosen school of magic. A school familiar cannot have any other familiar archetype (see page 10). At the GM's discretion, other schools of magic (such as elemental arcane schools from *Pathfinder RPG Ultimate Magic*) may have their own school familiars.

School Link (Su): A school familiar can use the share spells and deliver touch spells abilities only with spells of its master's specialized arcane school.

School Cantrip (Sp): A school familiar can cast at will one cantrip selected from its associated arcane school, using its master's caster level.

Specialty Stowaway (Sp or Su): A school familiar can use any granted abilities of its master's arcane school that have a limited number of uses or rounds per day, expending twice the number of uses or rounds as usual.

Lesser School Power: A school familiar gains the lesser school power matching its associated arcane school.

Greater School Power: A school familiar whose master has taken the Greater School Familiar feat gains the indicated greater school power of its associated arcane school.

Abjuration

An abjurer's familiar is an invaluable defensive aid.

Lesser—Energy Block (Su): Choose an energy type: acid, cold, electricity, fire, or sonic. The familiar gains energy resistance equal to 1/2 its master's level (minimum 1) to the chosen energy type and can share this resistance with one ally within 5 feet. As a standard action, the familiar's master can change this energy type. The familiar is immune to *magic missile* as if protected by *shield*.

Greater—Disruptive Spirit (Su): Whenever the familiar hits a creature with a natural attack, that creature is subject to a targeted *dispel magic* effect at the master's caster level. This ability can't be used while delivering a touch spell, and can't affect the same creature more than once in 24 hours.

Conjuration

Conjurers' familiars are masters of teleportation that can inhabit the bodies of summoned creatures.

Lesser—Master's Side (Sp): The familiar can use *dimension door* to return to its master's side a number of times per day equal to 3 + its Intelligence modifier (minimum once per day).

Greater—Summoned Shell (Sp): Whenever the familiar's master casts a *summon monster* spell, if the familiar is within the spell's range, it can choose to inhabit the body of one creature summoned by the spell. While inhabiting the body, the familiar maintains its own Intelligence, Wisdom, and Charisma scores and its familiar powers, but otherwise gains the statistics and abilities of the summoned creature. When the spell ends, or the summoned creature's hit points are reduced to 0, the familiar is expelled without suffering any negative effects.

Divination

A diviner's familiar complements its master's prescience.

Lesser—Ever Ready (Su): At the start of combat, the familiar and its master each roll initiative separately, and the master can choose to trade his initiative result with his familiar's. The familiar gains the benefits of the diviner's forewarned school power and can always act on the surprise round.

Greater—Greater Scry on Familiar (Sp): The master gains the scry on familiar ability (if he doesn't already possess it), and can use it at will as *greater scrying*.

Enchantment

Enchanters' familiars are devious manipulators capable of aiding in charms and compulsions.

Lesser—Manipulative Abettor (Su): If the familiar's master casts an enchantment spell while targeting a creature whose square is also occupied by his familiar, the save DC of the spell is increased by 2.

Greater—Puppet Master (Su): The familiar can strongly influence a creature through physical contact. Once per day, the familiar can make a melee touch attack against a creature and force it to make a Will save (DC = 10 + 1/2 the familiar's Hit Dice + its Charisma modifier) or be affected as if by *charm monster*. The effect lasts for as long as the familiar remains conscious and within 5 feet of the target (to a maximum of 24 hours). As soon as the effect ends, the freed victim is forever immune to that familiar's puppet master ability.

Evocation

Evocation familiars boost and manipulate energy spells.

Lesser—Energy Boost (Su): Choose an energy type: acid, cold, electricity, or fire. The familiar gains resistance 10 to the selected energy type. Whenever an ally casts an evocation spell that has the chosen energy type as a descriptor while within 5 feet of the familiar, the spell deals bonus energy damage equal to its spell level.

Greater—Eldritch Battery (Su): The familiar becomes immune to the energy type chosen for its energy boost ability. If the familiar's master casts an evocation spell that has that energy type as a descriptor, and targets the familiar or includes it in the spell's area, the familiar can choose to absorb the spell. Instead of the spell's normal effect, the familiar gains the spell (including any metamagic feats applied to it) as a spell-like ability. It can use this ability once, at half the spell's original caster level. If the halved caster level is insufficient to cast a spell of that level, the familiar doesn't gain the spell as a spell-like ability. The effect fades after 1 minute if not used.

Illusion

Illusion school familiars can control their master's illusions and create impressive illusions of their own.

Lesser—Illusory Maestro (Su): As a move action, the familiar's master can transfer control of any illusion spell that requires concentration to the familiar. The familiar's affinity for illusions also enhances the quality of the illusion, increasing the illusion's save DC (if any) by 1 for as long as the familiar concentrates on the spell.

Greater—Phantom Swarm (Su): As a standard action, the familiar can conjure hundreds of illusory duplicates of itself. The familiar can direct the phantom swarm as a normal swarm by moving along with it. The familiar gains a swarm attack that deals 1d6 points of damage with a distraction DC equal to 10 + the familiar's Constitution modifier. Opponents who fail to disbelieve the effect (Will DC = 10 + 1/2 the master's level + the familiar's Charisma modifier) treat the familiar as if it had the swarm subtype. The familiar takes any damage dealt to the swarm, including extra damage from area attacks, though it takes only half damage from slashing and piercing weapons. Creatures who successfully disbelieve the swarm are immune to the swarm's effects and can target the familiar as an individual creature. Only Tiny or smaller familiars can use this ability. This is an illusion (shadow) effect.

Necromancy

Necromancers' familiars are scions of undeath.

Lesser—Spirit Warden (Su): Whenever the familiar successfully uses aid another to aid an attack, that attack deals full damage to incorporeal creatures. When encountering a haunt, the familiar always acts on the surprise round, and can make touch attacks against the haunt that deal 1d6 points of damage per 2 levels its master possesses.

Greater—One With the Negative (Su): The familiar is healed by negative energy as if undead. It is immune to energy drain. It's constantly affected by *hide from undead*; if it breaks this effect by attacking, it can activate the effect again as a standard action. Whenever the familiar hits a living creature with a natural attack, that creature gains 1 negative level. A given creature can receive a negative level from the familiar only once per day.

Transmutation

A transmutation familiar is capable of protecting its master's effects as well as shapeshifting.

Lesser—Dispel Bait (Su): As a standard action, the familiar's master can expend a spell or an open spell slot to imbue the familiar with the ability to protect his transmutations. Whenever one of the master's transmutations would be successfully dispelled, if the familiar is within 10 feet of the transmutation effect and the imbued spell slot is of a level equal to or higher than the transmutation, the familiar can choose to lose the imbued spell slot to prevent the transmutation effect from being dispelled. The familiar can be imbued with only one dispel bait effect at a time.

Greater—Infinite Forms (Su): Once per day as a standard action, the familiar can transform into any animal familiar (but not an improved familiar), losing all of its racial abilities and becoming a typical familiar of the chosen type, including granting a different familiar bonus to its master.

Other Familiar Options

The following options provide characters with a variety of ways to make their familiars more versatile and central to the characters' themes.

Bloodline Familiars

Those with an inherent connection to magic often attract creatures who feel a similar instinctive pull toward magical forces. At 1st level, a sorcerer, bloodrager, or any other character with one of the following bloodlines can choose to gain a bloodline familiar. The character gains a familiar (as a wizard's familiar), treating her class level as her wizard level for the purposes of this ability. This familiar has an additional ability listed below based on the master's bloodline.

This replaces the 1st-level bloodline power granted by the character's bloodline; in addition, the character gains bonus spells from her bloodline one level later than she normally would. For example, a sorcerer with the aberrant bloodline who takes a bloodline familiar would not gain the acidic ray bloodline power, and she would gain her first bonus spell at 4th level, her second bonus spell at 6th level, and so on.

GMs may use the following bloodline familiar abilities as written, or employ them as guidelines for devising bloodline familiar abilities for bloodlines not listed below.

Aberrant—Squeezer (Ex): The familiar gains the compression ability, allowing it to move through an area as small as one-quarter its space without squeezing or one-eighth its space when squeezing.

Abyssal—Grotesque Appendages (Ex): The damage dice of each of the familiar's natural attacks increases by one die step.

Arcane—Spell Catalyst (Su): Spells you cast that target your familiar are treated as having a caster level 2 levels higher than your actual caster level.

Celestial—Heavenly Touch (Su): A number of times per day equal to 3 + your Charisma modifier, your familiar can grant fast healing 1 to an allied creature it's touching. This effect lasts a number of rounds equal to your Charisma modifier (minimum 1) or until the familiar stops touching the creature, whichever comes first. At 10th level, the familiar grants fast healing 2 instead. At 20th level, the familiar grants fast healing 3 instead.

Destined—Foretold Touch (Su): The familiar gains a +1 luck bonus on attack rolls to deliver touch spells, and the DC of touch spells delivered by the familiar increases by 1. These benefits increase by 1 at 10th level and again at 20th level.

Draconic—Dragon's Flight (Ex): The familiar can sprout draconic wings, granting it a fly speed of 30 feet with average maneuverability for a number of minutes per day equal to 1/2 your caster level (minimum 1). These minutes need not be consecutive, but they must be spent in 1-minute increments. At 10th level, the familiar's fly speed increases to 60 feet with good maneuverability. At 20th level, the familiar's fly speed increases to 90 feet.

Elemental—Dualistic Energy (Su): When your familiar delivers a touch spell that deals energy damage of a type other than your chosen energy type, your familiar can choose to alter the spell so that half of the energy damage dealt is of the spell's original type and the other half is of your chosen energy type.

Fey—Amusing Familiar (Su): The familiar can fascinate other creatures as the fascinate bardic performance, treating your caster level as its bard level and using your Charisma modifier for the purpose of calculating the Will save DC. The familiar cannot perform any other actions while using this ability.

Infernal—Hellish Aura (Su): Animals don't willingly approach the familiar unless the animal's master succeeds at a DC 15 Handle Animal, Ride, or wild empathy check. This DC increases to 20 at 10th level, and to 25 at 20th level. Animal companions, familiars and mounts are immune to this effect.

Undead—Unliving Physiology (Su): The familiar is alive, but is treated as undead for all effects that affect undead differently from living creatures, such as cure spells and channeled energy.

Patron Familiars

Witches' familiars are often tied to their patrons, enhancing and reinforcing the spellcasters' connections to the sources of their magical might. Just as a sorcerer can gain a bloodline familiar, a witch can gain a patron familiar by choosing one at 1st level in place of her standard familiar. A patron familiar acts in all ways like a standard witch's familiar, with the addition of the special ability indicated below according to the witch's patron. In addition, the witch gains her patron spells 1 level later than she normally would—gaining the patron spell she'd normally receive at 2nd level at 3rd level instead, and so on.

Agility—Supernatural Speed (Su): The familiar is incredibly fast for its type. It gains an enhancement bonus of +10 feet to each of its movement speeds. This bonus increases to +20 feet at 10th level, and to +30 feet at 20th level.

Animals—Animal Speaker (Su): The familiar gains the ability to speak with animals of its kind at 1st level. If it would normally gain this ability at 7th level, the familiar gains the ability to speak with all animals (as though constantly under the effects of *speak with animals*) at 7th level.

Deception—Distracting (Su and Sp): The familiar gains Bluff and Sense Motive as class skills. At 10th level, the familiar can throw its voice at will, as if using *ventriloquism*.

Elements—Elemental Touch (Su): Choose an energy type: acid, cold, electricity, or fire. The familiar gains resistance 5 to the selected energy type. Whenever the familiar delivers a touch spell that deals energy damage, it can change the type of energy damage dealt to the selected energy type.

Endurance—Endure Afflictions (Su): The familiar is unnaturally talented at resisting bodily corruption. The familiar and any ally touching it gains a +2 resistance bonus on saving throws against nonmagical poisons and diseases. At 10th level, this bonus also applies against magical diseases and poisons. At 20th level, this bonus also applies against curses.

Plague—Diseased Touch (Ex): Once per day, the familiar can inflict filth fever with its natural attacks for 1 round. At 10th level, the familiar can inflict red ache instead. At 20th level, it can inflict demon fever instead. See page 557 of the *Pathfinder RPG Core Rulebook* for details on these diseases. The familiar may be able to inflict other injury diseases instead at the GM's discretion.

Shadow—Fearsome Shadows (Sp): Once per day, the familiar can use *cause fear* as a spell-like ability as long as it is in an area of normal or dim light, affecting a single living creature with a number of Hit Dice up to the familiar's Intelligence score. Thus, creatures normally immune to *cause fear* because they have 6 or more Hit Dice may not be immune to the familiar's *cause fear* spell-like ability.

Strength—Strength of Mind (Su): A number of times per day equal to its master's Intelligence modifier (minimum once per day), the familiar can swap its Strength and Intelligence scores as a standard action. This effect lasts for a number of rounds equal to 1/2 the master's caster level.

Transformation—Shapechanging Familiar (Su): The familiar is able to transform itself. For a number of minutes per day equal to its master's witch level, the familiar can alter its appearance so that it looks like a different creature of its type and size. The duration doubles at 8th level, and triples at 16th level. This duration need not be consecutive, but it must be used in 1 minute increments. For instance, a cat familiar could appear as any Tiny animal. This change is purely cosmetic, and doesn't alter the familiar's statistics.

Trickery—Familiar's Illusions (Sp): The familiar has a mischievous predilection toward simple illusions. Once per day, the familiar can use a 0-level illusion spell on its master's spell list as a spell-like ability. At 10th level, it can also use a 1st-level illusion spell on its master's spell list once per day. At 20th level, it can also use a 2nd-level illusion spell on its master's spell list once per day.

Water—Amphibious Familiar (Su): The familiar can breathe water for a number of minutes per day equal to 1/2 its master's witch level. These minutes need not be consecutive, but they must be spent in 1-minute intervals. If the familiar can already breathe water, it can breathe air for the same duration. At 10th level, the familiar gains a swim speed of 30 feet (or a land speed of 30 feet if it already has a swim speed) while using this ability. At 20th level, the familiar can move through water as though under the effects of *freedom of movement* while using this ability.

Wisdom—Preternatural Wisdom (Su): The familiar gains a Wisdom score of 6. This score increases by 1 point at 3rd level and every 2 levels thereafter (at the same rate as its Intelligence score). This may cause a familiar whose Wisdom score is typically higher than 6 to start with a lower Wisdom score than normal.

Familiar Feats

This section presents new feats for characters with familiars. Additionally, the new Familiar Bond feat allows any character to gain a familiar, regardless of class.

Master Feats

Characters who meet the prerequisites can take the following feats to make further use of their familiars.

Familiar Bond

You have learned a ritual that allows you to gain a familiar.

Prerequisite: Iron Will.

Benefit: You gain a familiar, as the wizard arcane bond class feature. You do not gain the special ability the familiar normally grants its master, and the familiar does not gain the deliver touch spells, scry on familiar, share spells, speak with animals of its kind, or spell resistance special abilities. Otherwise, your total Hit Dice are used as your wizard level for determining the familiar's abilities.

Special: If you have (or later gain) levels in a class that grants a familiar, whenever you select a familiar, you can either base your familiar's abilities on your total Hit Dice per this feat (including the restrictions on its special abilities), or choose to apply only your levels in classes that grant a familiar (and thus gain all the special abilities that familiar would grant based on those class levels). You can never have more than one familiar.

Far-Roaming Familiar

Distance can't sever the bond between you and your familiar.

Prerequisites: Intelligence 13, must have a familiar.

Benefit: You retain your empathic link to your familiar regardless of distance, though lead blocks the link at distances greater than 1 mile (similar to the way lead blocks *detect magic* effects).

Group Deliver Touch Spells (Teamwork)

You and your teammates can deliver touch spells through each other's familiars.

Prerequisites: Group Shared Spells, must have a familiar with the share spells and deliver touch spells abilities.

Benefit: You and any allies with this feat can cast spells through one another's familiars as though each ally had the share spells ability with each other familiar. This feat otherwise functions as the share spells ability.

Group Shared Spells (Teamwork)

Your allies can cast spells through each other's familiars.

Prerequisite: Must have a familiar with the share spells ability.

Benefit: You and any allies with this feat can cast spells with a target of "you" on each other's familiars as touch spells. Both the target familiar and that familiar's master must be willing for the spell to take effect. You can cast spells on each other's familiars even if the spells would not normally affect creatures of the targeted familiar's type.

Improved Familiar Bond

Your familiar gains greater power.

Prerequisites: Familiar Bond, Iron Will.

Benefit: Your familiar gains all the normal abilities available to a familiar of a wizard with a level equal to your total Hit Dice. You also gain the special ability normally gained by a master of your type of familiar.

Telepathic Link

You can telepathically communicate with your familiar.

Prerequisite: Must have a familiar with the speak with master ability.

Benefit: You and your familiar can communicate with each other telepathically at a range of up to 1 mile.

Familiar Feats

The following feats can be taken by characters who have familiars that meet the listed prerequisites. Wizards can take a familiar feat as a bonus feat, and witches can select a familiar feat in place of a hex. If you lose your familiar and gain a new familiar that doesn't meet the listed prerequisites for a familiar feat you possess, your new familiar doesn't gain the benefits of that feat. A new familiar that meets the prerequisites automatically gains the benefits of that feat.

When you gain a new level, if your current familiar does not meet the prerequisite of a familiar feat you possess, you can learn a new familiar feat in place of the feat your familiar doesn't qualify for. In effect, you lose the old familiar feat in exchange for the new one. The feat lost can't be a prerequisite for another feat you possess, and your familiar must meet the new feat's prerequisites. You can exchange only one feat in this way each time you gain a level.

Decoy's Misdirection (Familiar)

You can fool scrying attempts by using your familiar.

Prerequisite: Must have a familiar with the decoy archetype (see page 10).

Benefit: As long as your familiar is within 30 feet of you, anytime you succeed at a Will save to negate a scrying effect (including *scrying* and *greater scrying*), you become aware of the scrying attempt as though you succeeded at the Spellcraft check to identify it, and you can choose to let the spell function as normal instead of causing it to fail. If you do, you can choose to redirect the scrying effect toward your familiar, causing the familiar to immediately change shape (as its secret sharer spell-like ability, except the duration is as long as the scrying effect lasts). The creator of the scrying effect observes the familiar as though it were you, though spells such as *detect magic* detect the *alter self* effect as normal.

Emissary's Emboldening (Familiar)

Your familiar lends you divine courage.

Prerequisite: Must have a familiar with the emissary archetype (see page 10).

Benefit: As long as your familiar is adjacent to you, you gain a +1 morale bonus against fear effects. This bonus increases by 1 at 4th level and every 4 levels thereafter (to a maximum of +5 at 16th level). At 20th level, you become immune to fear effects as long as your familiar is adjacent to you.

Figment's Fluidity (Familiar)

Your familiar can rework the dream-stuff it is made of.

Prerequisite: Must have a familiar with the figment archetype (see page 10).

Benefit: Once per day, your familiar can spend a full-round action to manually reshape itself, reassigning 1 evolution point of eidolon evolutions. The evolution it loses can't be a prerequisite for any other evolutions it has. It can use this ability twice per day at 7th level, and three times per day at 13th level.

Guardian's Return (Familiar)

Your familiar can teleport to you when you're in need.

Prerequisite: Must have a familiar with the protector archetype (see page 11).

Benefit: Once per day when you take damage from a melee attack, as long as your familiar is within empathic link range, it can teleport back to your square as an immediate action. It can bring no more than 5 pounds of items with it when it teleports in this way. This ability otherwise functions as *dimension door*.

Mascot's Affection (Familiar)

Your familiar can bond with many creatures.

Prerequisite: Must have a familiar with the mascot archetype (see page 11).

Benefit: The maximum number of team members your familiar can have increases by two.

Mauler's Endurance (Familiar)

Your familiar is harder to kill than most.

Prerequisite: Must have a familiar with the mauler archetype (see page 11).

Benefit: Your familiar gains 2 hit points per level you possess.

Polyglot Familiar (Familiar)

Your familiar can speak with animals other than those of its own kind.

Prerequisite: Must have a familiar.

Benefit: Choose a category of creature: amphibians, birds, felines, invertebrates, reptiles, rodents, simians, or vermin. Your familiar can speak with creatures of that kind.

Special: This feat can be taken multiple times, choosing a different category of creature each time. The first time you take this feat, if your familiar can't already speak with creatures of its kind, you must choose that category of creature. If your familiar later gains the ability to speak with creatures of its kind, you can choose to apply this feat's benefits to a different category of creature instead.

Sage's Guidance (Familiar)

Your familiar's keen observations help you defeat foes.

Prerequisite: Must have a familiar with the sage archetype (see page 11).

Benefit: When your familiar succeeds at a Knowledge check to identify a hazard or an opponent's weaknesses and abilities, you gain a +2 insight bonus on attacks and skill checks against the opponent or hazard for 1 round. If your familiar is sharing a space with the opponent or hazard, this bonus is granted to all allies who can see and understand the familiar.

Equipment & Magic Items

Spellcasters the world over have developed a variety of useful tools, gadgets, and other equipment to fortify their own familiars or exploit the weaknesses of rivals'.

New Equipment

The following new items increase the efficacy or versatility of familiars.

AQUARIUM BALL	PRICE 80 GP
	WEIGHT 20 lbs.

This clear, 1-inch-thick glass orb is the size of a large melon and hangs from a thick chain. It can hold up to 2 gallons of freshwater or saltwater, allowing it to house aquatic creatures such as fish or frogs. The cap near the top of the ball can be unscrewed for access. One Tiny creature or two Diminutive creatures can fit comfortably into an aquarium ball. The water within the orb must be changed daily in order to keep the creatures within alive. Otherwise, the inhabitants begin to slowly suffocate (see page 445 of the *Pathfinder RPG Core Rulebook*).

BEAST WHISTLE	PRICE 5 GP
	WEIGHT —

This small wooden whistle emits a high-pitched sound like that of a signal whistle, except the signal is audible only to a specific type of creature—other types of creatures hear only a quiet hissing sound.

Beast whistles come in six different varieties: avian, canine, feline, rodent, reptile, and ungulate (other varieties may be available at the GM's discretion). Animals and magical beasts that match a beast whistle's type can hear the whistle as a human hears a signal whistle. Creatures that fit into multiple categories (such as griffons) can usually hear the call of multiple types of whistles, though magical beasts who don't fit into any of the above categories cannot hear a beast whistle. Beast whistles don't function underwater, except if surrounded by an *air bubble* (*Pathfinder RPG Ultimate Combat* 222) or similar effect, though creatures underwater may hear a beast whistle sounded from above the surface if they are close enough.

HIDE DYE	PRICE 20 GP
	WEIGHT 1 lb.

This thick, murky liquid comes in a large earthenware jug, and can be purchased in a variety of colors. Hide dye can be applied to the feathers, fur, scales, or skin of most types of animals and magical beasts, allowing creatures a measure of camouflage. Hide dye comes in a variety of colors and shades matching the following different kinds of terrain: cold (including ice, glaciers, snow, and tundra), desert, forest, jungle, mountain (including hills), plains, swamp, underground, urban, and water.

One jar of hide dye can be applied to a Small or smaller animal or magical beast in 1 hour. Thereafter, the dyed creature gains a +2 circumstance bonus on Stealth checks in the associated terrain. If the Environment entry in a creature's statistics indicates that the creature can typically be found in a specific type of terrain (such as an owl's environment of temperate forests) and the creature is adorned with hide dye of a matching type, the bonus on Stealth checks increases to +4. Applying a new color of dye immediately covers and replaces the previous dye.

Hide dye doesn't adhere to clothing or humanoid flesh, and grants no benefit to creatures other than animals or magical beasts. Once applied, hide dye is waterproof and can't be rubbed or burned away. It fades after 1d4+1 days unless it's removed earlier by magical means.

New Drugs and Poisons

The following drugs and poisons can be useful for enhancing or subduing familiars' behaviors.

CATNIP	PRICE 5 GP

Type ingested; **Addiction** minor, **Fortitude** DC 11
Effects 1d6 minutes (felines only); +1 alchemical bonus on initiative checks, +2 alchemical bonus on Reflex saves
Effect after 1d6 minutes; fatigued for 1d3 hours
Damage 1 Wis damage

Catnip (also known as catswort or catmint) is a flowering type of mint plant that grows abundantly throughout Southern Avistan and the jungles of Garund. To felines, catnip is a stimulant that increases pleasure and reaction times. Once the stimulating effects have worn off, an affected feline becomes sluggish for several hours, and must wait until the sluggishness wears off before it can gain the benefits of catnip again. Even large felines such as lions and tigers react to catnip, though they may need a larger dose to be affected. Catnip has no effect whatsoever on any creatures except felines.

HAZEMIND CONCENTRATE	PRICE 200 GP

Type poison, injury; **Save** Fortitude DC 16
Onset 1 round; **Frequency** 1/round for 6 rounds
Effects The subject's mind goes fuzzy, shifting its attitudes toward all other creatures one step closer to indifferent; DCs to influence the subject with Charisma, Diplomacy, Handle Animal, or Intimidate checks increase by 4; **Cure** 1 save

HAZEMIND MIST	PRICE 225 GP

Type poison, inhaled; **Save** Fortitude DC 13
Onset 1 round; **Frequency** 1/round for 10 rounds
Effects as hazemind concentrate (see above); **Cure** 1 save

Magic Items

The following magic items include aids for spellcasters with familiars and a useful weapon against enemies' bonded creatures.

FEATHERLEAF BARDING		PRICE 7,310 GP
SLOT armor	CL 9th	WEIGHT 1 lb.
AURA faint transmutation		

This enchanted sleeve is made of tiny, feather-shaped leaves and is designed to fit birds. Once fitted over the body of a Tiny or smaller avian creature, *featherleaf barding* automatically shrinks to snugly fit the creature's torso and neck, serving as *+1 leather armor* (granting a total bonus to AC of +2). The maximum fly speed of a creature wearing *featherleaf barding* is 60 feet with average maneuverability. In forests, jungles, and thickly wooded areas, the wearer can fly through branches, brush, and even whole tree trunks as if they weren't there, though its fly speed and maneuverability remain the same.

CONSTRUCTION REQUIREMENTS	COST 3,660 GP
Craft Magic Arms and Armor, *fly*, *tree stride*	

GLOVE OF FAMILIAR'S TOUCH		PRICE 23,000 GP
SLOT hands	CL 7th	WEIGHT 2 lbs.
AURA moderate evocation		

A *glove of familiar's touch* features a large, brightly colored gem fastened to its palm, and comes with an additional gem attuned to the glove. As long as his familiar is touching the attuned gem, the wearer of this glove can designate his familiar as the source for any touch spell he casts, even if he and his familiar are not in contact when the spell is cast. A *glove of familiar's touch* takes up the wearer's entire hands slot; the wearer can't gain the benefits of another magic item (even another *glove of familiar's touch*) that also uses the hands slot.

CONSTRUCTION REQUIREMENTS	COST 11,500 GP
Craft Wondrous Item, *imbue with spell ability*	

MUNDANITY GREASE		PRICE 500 GP
SLOT none	CL 11th	WEIGHT 1 lb.
AURA moderate abjuration		

This slippery, jet-black goo has a consistency comparable to warm lard. A bottle of *mundanity grease* can be thrown as a splash weapon with a range increment of 10 feet.

When an animal companion, a familiar, or another bonded creature is struck by *mundanity grease*, the bond to its master is temporarily suspended. The creature and its master lose any of the following abilities they have from the companion or familiar bond: deliver touch spells, devotion, empathic link, evasion, improved evasion, link, scry on familiar, share spells, speak with animals of its kind, spell resistance, and speak with master. For the duration of the effect, a familiar originally of the animal type is treated as an animal (rather than a magical beast) for the purposes of determining which spells affect it. This effect lasts for 1d4 minutes or until the grease is washed off the affected creature by magical means.

CONSTRUCTION REQUIREMENTS	COST 250 GP
Craft Wondrous Item, *greater dispel magic*	

REPLENISHING AQUARIUM BALL	PRICE varies
Lesser	500 GP
Standard	2,000 GP
Greater	4,000 GP

SLOT none	CL 7th	WEIGHT 20 lbs.
AURA moderate conjuration		

Replenishing aquarium balls act as standard aquarium balls (see page 20), but are endowed with magical effects beneficial to the creature held within. The power of the magic depends on the kind of *replenishing aquarium ball*.

Lesser: The ball continually refreshes itself with clean water, allowing a creature within to live as long as it has food.

Standard: The ball continually refreshes itself with clean water and fresh food.

Greater: The ball continually refreshes itself with clean water and fresh food. In addition, a *greater replenishing aquarium ball* is magically enhanced so that the glass is as hard as stone (hardness 8, 15 hp) without increasing its weight.

CONSTRUCTION REQUIREMENTS	COST varies
Lesser	250 GP
Standard	1,000 GP
Greater	2,000 GP

Craft Wondrous Item; *create water* (lesser); *create food and water* (standard); *create food and water*, *stoneskin* (greater)

SPELL-SHARING COLLAR		PRICE 7,500 GP
SLOT neck	CL 10th	WEIGHT 1 lb.
AURA moderate evocation		

This thick leather collar is studded with onyx gems and fastened with a simple metal clasp. *Spell-sharing collars* come in a variety of sizes and can be secured around the neck of any creature capable of wearing and using a neck-slot item. They are usually sold in sets.

A creature with the share spells ability (such as an animal companion or familiar) wearing a *spell-sharing collar* can benefit from that ability with any other creature wearing such a collar that is attuned to its own collar, rather than gaining the benefit only with its bonded master. Attuning two or more *spell-sharing collars* takes 10 minutes, during which time the collars must be touching one another. A *spell-sharing collar* can have as many as three other *spell-sharing collars* attuned to it at once. The granted ability otherwise functions as a familiar's share spells ability.

CONSTRUCTION REQUIREMENTS	COST 3,750 GP
Craft Wondrous Items, *imbue with spell ability*	

Spells

Word is spreading among arcane scholars about the original spells of one Erilen Balestis, a mystic theurge of Nethys. The singular intensity of Balestis's focus on the topic of familiars is matched only by the extraordinary diversity of his approaches to it. Below are some of Balestis's more recent discoveries, currently circulating among spellcasters the world over, especially among the church of the All-Seeing Eye.

CALLBACK

School conjuration (teleportation); **Level** bard 2, druid 2, sorcerer/wizard 2, witch 2
Casting Time 1 standard action
Components V, S, M (crushed grasshopper)

Range long (400 ft. + 40 ft./level)
Target your familiar
Duration 10 minutes/level or until expended (see text)
Saving Throw Fortitude negates (harmless); **Spell Resistance** yes (harmless)

If your familiar takes hit point damage while within range of this spell, it immediately teleports to your space after the damage is applied. If it's killed, its corpse teleports instead. Optionally, you can specify a number of points of damage for your familiar to take before the spell takes effect. Once the familiar has teleported back to you, the spell ends.

CALLBACK, GREATER

School conjuration (teleportation); **Level** bard 5, druid 5, sorcerer/wizard 5, witch 5
Range 1 mile/level
Duration 1 hour/level or until expended
This spell functions as *callback*, except as noted above.

DISRUPT LINK

School abjuration; **Level** antipaladin 2, bard 3, inquisitor 3, sorcerer/wizard 2, witch 2
Casting Time 1 standard action
Components V, S
Range medium (100 ft. + 10 ft./level)
Targets one creature and her animal companion, familiar, or other bonded creature (which may be no more than 30 ft. apart)
Duration 1 round/level
Saving Throw Will negates; **Spell Resistance** yes

The target has her link with her bonded creature temporarily severed. If the subject has a familiar, she loses the benefits of the alertness, deliver touch spells, empathic link, scry on familiar, share spells, and speak with master abilities. If the target has an animal companion, she loses the benefits of the link, share spells, and devotion abilities. The target and her familiar or animal companion also lose any other abilities (such as those from archetypes or feats) that rely on the two having a connection.

DUPLICATE FAMILIAR

School conjuration (creation); **Level** alchemist 4, sorcerer/wizard 5, witch 5
Casting Time 1 standard action
Components V, S, M (alchemically preserved mockingfey feathers), F (familiar)
Range touch
Effect temporary duplicate of familiar touched
Duration 10 minutes/level
Saving Throw Fortitude negates; **Spell Resistance** no

You create a duplicate of a familiar. The familiar's master can use the duplicate as if it were his familiar in all respects, though he doesn't gain the bonus special ability from more

OTHER SPELLS

In addition to the new spells in this book, spellcasters seeking to maximize the synergy between their spells and their familiars may consider the following spells from *Pathfinder Player Companion: Animal Archive* and other sources.

Spell	Level	Source
Bleed for your master	Antipaladin 2, druid 4, ranger 3, sorcerer/wizard 3, witch 3	*Animal Archive* 24
Die for your master	Antipaladin 4, druid 5, sorcerer/wizard 5, witch 5	*Animal Archive* 24
Familiar figment	Sorcerer/wizard 2, witch 2	*Animal Archive* 24
Familiar melding	Sorcerer/wizard 4, witch 4	*Ultimate Magic* 219
Raise animal companion	Druid 5, paladin 4, ranger 4	*Ultimate Magic* 233
Share senses	Sorcerer/wizard 4, witch 3	*Advanced Player's Guide* 243
Share shape	Ranger 3, sorcerer/wizard 4, witch 4	*Animal Archive* 25
Shield companion	Antipaladin 1, druid 1, paladin 1, ranger 1, sorcerer/wizard 1, witch 1	*Animal Archive* 25

than one familiar at a time. When the spell's duration expires, the familiar duplicate shrivels into nothing, even if petrified or otherwise transformed.

EMPATHY CONDUIT

School necromancy; **Level** shaman 5, sorcerer/wizard 5, witch 5
Casting Time 1 standard action
Components V, S, F (a glass rod)
Range medium (100 ft. + 10 ft./level)
Targets an animal companion, familiar, or other bonded creature and its master (which may be no more than 30 ft. apart)
Duration 1 round/level
Saving Throw Will negates; **Spell Resistance** yes

You make a conduit between the targeted master and her familiar, allowing you to target the master or the familiar with your spells in order to affect the other. If the master succeeds at its save to resist this spell but the familiar fails, you can choose to have your spells that target the master affect the familiar instead. If the familiar resists but the master doesn't, your spells that target the familiar can affect the master instead. If both the familiar and the master fail to resist this spell, you can affect either the familiar or the master when you target either with a spell. When you target the master to affect her familiar or vice versa, the target attempts a save (if one is allowed) with its own saving throw bonus, but the other creature is affected by the spell.

Only spells that target one or more creatures can be cast through *empathy conduit*. The creature to be affected must still be a valid target of the spell being cast; for example, you can't affect a familiar with *charm person* through an *empathy conduit*. Spells with a duration other than instantaneous that are cast through an *empathy conduit* last either their normal duration or until the *empathy conduit* expires, whichever comes first. Whenever the master or its familiar is targeted with a spell intended to affect the other creature, the targeted creature can attempt an additional save against the *empathy conduit*.

MERGE WITH FAMILIAR

School transmutation; **Level** alchemist 2, sorcerer/wizard 2, witch 2
Casting Time 1 standard action
Components V, S
Range touch
Target your familiar

Duration 1 hour/level (D)
Saving Throw Fortitude negates (harmless); **Spell Resistance** yes (harmless)

Your familiar merges harmlessly into your body. For the duration of this spell, you or your familiar can separate or merge at will as a move action. While merged, your familiar can't be targeted or affected by any means (including ongoing effects).

SOULSWITCH

School necromancy; **Level** bard 5, cleric 5, druid 5, inquisitor 5, magus 5, shaman 5, sorcerer/wizard 5, witch 5
Casting Time 1 standard action
Components V, S, F (two brass collars worth 50 gp each)
Range touch
Targets you and your familiar
Duration 10 minutes/level
Saving Throw Will negates (harmless); **Spell Resistance** yes (harmless)

You may only cast this spell if you currently have a familiar. You place your soul into the body of your familiar, and your familiar's soul is placed in your body. This functions as if you possessed your familiar using *magic jar*; your familiar simultaneously possesses your body in the same manner. You can't freely transfer your soul between your body and your familiar's—if you choose to return to your body as a standard action, the spell ends. If either body is killed, both spirits return to their original bodies, the spell ends, and the original owner of the slain body dies.

TRANSFER FAMILIAR

School evocation; **Level** sorcerer/wizard 6, witch 6
Casting Time 1 standard action
Components V, S
Range touch
Target your familiar and one willing creature
Duration 1 day/level (D)
Saving Throw none; **Spell Resistance** no

You temporarily grant control of your familiar to another willing creature. You, your familiar, and the target creature must all be touching each other when you cast this spell. The target gains all the benefits and abilities normally associated with having a familiar, including the ability to share spells, speak with the familiar, and so on. You lose all of these benefits for the duration of the spell. If the target already has a familiar, the spell fails.

Tiny Animal Familiars

Golarion is full of diverse wildlife, with many creatures that can readily serve as adventurers' familiars. The following animals are just a few such beasts. The special abilities these familiars grant to their masters can be found on the inside front cover of this book.

Chicken

This fowl has a compact body, a short beak flanked by red wattles, and a crimson comb on the crown of its head.

CHICKEN	CR 1/6	

XP 65

N Tiny animal

Init +4; **Senses** low-light vision; Perception +5

DEFENSE

AC 12, touch 12, flat-footed 12 (+2 size)

hp 5 (1d8+1)

Fort +3, **Ref** +2, **Will** +1

OFFENSE

Speed 30 ft., fly 20 ft. (clumsy); drift

Melee bite –2 (1d3–4)

Space 2-1/2 ft.; **Reach** 0 ft.

STATISTICS

Str 3, **Dex** 11, **Con** 12, **Int** 2, **Wis** 12, **Cha** 13

Base Atk +0; **CMB** –2; **CMD** 4

Feats Improved Initiative

Skills Fly –4, Perception +5

SPECIAL ABILITIES

Drift (Ex) A chicken flies in short bursts, and can't use its fly speed to hover. When it flies, a chicken must end its move action by landing or perching on a solid surface.

While not particularly useful to travelers as combatants, chickens are prized for the hearty breakfast meals they provide if properly fed and cared for. Chickens are highly social creatures that raise their young communally. They're picky about the spots where they roost, and a hen rarely strays from a particular nest once she's laid her eggs there. A fertilized chicken egg hatches into a chick after roughly 3 weeks of incubation.

In addition to their quick reproductive cycles, chickens have the ability to thrive on simple foods, and they are valued in both rural farming communities and metropolitan areas for their delicious and nutrient-rich eggs and meat. A hen bred for laying eggs can produce up to one egg every 24 hours.

A chicken is about 1 foot tall and weighs 5 pounds.

Kakapo

This rotund parrot has vibrant green-and-black feathers, a short hooked beak, and an array of white whiskers around its face.

KAKAPO	CR 1/8	

XP 50

N Tiny animal

Init +1; **Senses** low-light vision; Perception +3

DEFENSE

AC 13, touch 13, flat-footed 12 (+1 Dex, +2 size)

hp 4 (1d8)

Fort +2, **Ref** +5, **Will** –1

OFFENSE

Speed 30 ft., climb 10 ft.; parachute

Melee bite –2 (1d3–4)

Space 2-1/2 ft.; **Reach** 0 ft.

STATISTICS

Str 3, **Dex** 13, **Con** 10, **Int** 1, **Wis** 8, **Cha** 12

Base Atk +0; **CMB** –1; **CMD** 5

Feats Lightning Reflexes

Skills Climb +4, Perception +3

ECOLOGY

Environment warm jungles or plains

Organization solitary, pair, or family (3–4)
Treasure none

SPECIAL ABILITIES

Parachute (Ex) Though it cannot fly, a kakapo can spread its wings mid-fall to parachute safely to the ground without taking damage. A kakapo never takes falling damage. For every 10 feet it falls, a kakapo can move 5 feet laterally in midair. For instance, a kakapo falling a vertical distance of 20 feet can move 10 feet laterally.

The kakapo is a small, flightless parrot native to the island nation of Minata just south of the continent of Tian Xia. Kakapos can live to be over 100 years old. They breed only two or three times per decade, when the rimu tree (their preferred food source) is most heavily fruiting. A kakapo is roughly 2 feet long from beak to tail tip and can weigh up to 9 pounds.

The people of Minata believe the kakapo to be a sacred animal, and some believe the bird has the ability to foretell the future. Tribal Minatans work images of the kakapo into their religious art, relating the bird to Shelyn, Pharasma, or one of their various tribal deities.

Mole

This brown, apparently eyeless rodent has a furry cylindrical body, a pointed snout, and large, thick paws that end in digging claws.

MOLE	CR 1/6	

XP 65

N Tiny animal

Init +0; **Senses** low-light vision; Perception +7

DEFENSE

AC 12, touch 12, flat-footed 12 (+2 size)

hp 6 (1d8+2)

Fort +4, **Ref** +2, **Will** +0

OFFENSE

Speed 20 ft., burrow 10 ft.

Melee claw –1 (1d2–3)

Space 2-1/2 ft.; **Reach** 0 ft.

STATISTICS

Str 5, **Dex** 11, **Con** 14, **Int** 2, **Wis** 10, **Cha** 7

Base Atk +0; **CMB** –2; **CMD** 5

Feats Skill Focus (Perception)

Skills Perception +7

SQ hold breath

ECOLOGY

Environment any land

Organization solitary, pair, or labor (3–5)

Treasure none

Moles are small rodent mammals that live primarily in burrows underground. While many varieties of moles exist, most share common features that include subterranean habitats, poor eyesight, and the ability to dig long distances with their powerful forelimbs. The typical mole is 6 inches long and weighs less than a pound. These familiars are popular choices with ratfolk.

Pufferfish

This spotted fish has pronounced eyes, a wide mouth, and tiny, brightly colored spikes protruding from its round body.

PUFFERFISH	CR 1/4	

XP 100

N Tiny animal (aquatic)

Init +2; **Senses** low-light vision; Perception +5

DEFENSE

AC 14, touch 14, flat-footed 12 (+2 Dex, +2 size)

hp 6 (1d8+2)

Fort +4, **Ref** +4, **Will** +1

Defensive Abilities spines

OFFENSE

Speed swim 20 ft.

MELEE

Space 2-1/2 ft.; **Reach** 0 ft.

Special Attacks poison

STATISTICS

Str 4, **Dex** 14, **Con** 15, **Int** 1, **Wis** 12, **Cha** 9

Base Atk +0; **CMB** +0; **CMD** 7

Feats Agile Maneuvers

Skills Perception +5, Swim +5

ECOLOGY

Environment warm coastlines

Organization solitary or school (2–8)

Treasure none

SPECIAL ABILITIES

Poison (Ex) *Tetrodotoxin*: Spines—injury; *save* Fort DC 12; *frequency* once; *initial effect* staggered for 1 round; *secondary effect* paralysis for 1d4 rounds; *cure* 2 consecutive saves. The save DC is Constitution-based.

Spines (Ex) Pufferfish aren't equipped attack other creatures, but foes that strike a pufferfish with an unarmed strike or natural attack risk being poisoned by the fish's toxic spines, and must immediately save against the pufferfish's tetrodotoxin.

Pufferfish (or "puffers") are a category of poisonous fish that dwell in warm coastal waters. Pufferfish have the ability to rapidly fill their stomachs with water or air, causing their bodies to balloon out and make the poisonous spikes on their skin more pronounced. While certain aquatic sharks and other animals have adapted to eat pufferfish, the puffer's tetrodotoxin (typically delivered via the spines on the fish's skin, though prevalent throughout its organs as well) remains highly poisonous to humans and most mammals. Puffers come in a large variety of sizes and varieties, and most range from 6 inches to 2 feet in length and weigh between 5 and 30 pounds.

Certain societies in Tian Xia (particularly in the coastal regions of Minkai) regard pufferfish meat as a delicacy. The specially trained chefs capable of reliably distinguishing the poisonous parts of the pufferfish from the nontoxic parts are highly prized by members of Tian nobility.

Small Animal Familiars

The following new types of animals hail from remote lands far from the Inner Sea region. The special abilities granted by these familiars to their masters can be found on the inside front cover of this book. See the Unusual Familiars sidebar on page 31 for more on having Small familiars.

Dolphin, Popoto

This sleek mammal has a short snout and black, white, and gray markings along its body, with a rounded black dorsal fin.

POPOTO	CR 1/3	

XP 135

N Small animal

Init +3; **Senses** blindsight 60 ft., low-light vision; Perception +5

DEFENSE

AC 15, touch 14, flat-footed 12 (+3 Dex, +1 natural, +1 size)

hp 4 (1d8)

Fort +2, **Ref** +5, **Will** +1

OFFENSE

Speed swim 60 ft.

Melee slam +4 (1d3–1)

STATISTICS

Str 8, **Dex** 17, **Con** 11, **Int** 2, **Wis** 13, **Cha** 6

Base Atk +0; **CMB** –1; **CMD** 12

Feats Weapon Finesse

Skills Perception +5, Swim +7

SQ hold breath

SPECIAL ABILITIES

Hold Breath (Ex) A popoto can hold its breath for a number of minutes equal to 6 times its Constitution score before it risks drowning.

Popotos are the smallest breed of dolphin, and generally swim in shallow waters near shorelines. They are social hunters, traveling in small groups called pods, which normally contain three to five popotos. Like larger dolphins, popotos are popular with seafarers, who consider the creatures good luck and tell tales of popotos leading lost swimmers to shore and pods fighting off sharks much larger than themselves.

Koala

This wide-faced animal looks like a small, plump bear, with a flat black nose, small round eyes, and white-tufted ears that protrude from the sides of its head.

KOALA	CR 1/4	

XP 100

N Small animal

Init +0; **Senses** low-light vision; Perception +3

DEFENSE

AC 11, touch 11, flat-footed 11 (+1 size)

hp 5 (1d8+1)

Fort +3, **Ref** +2, **Will** –1

OFFENSE

Speed 20 ft., climb 20 ft.

Melee 2 claws +1 (1d3–2)

STATISTICS

Str 6, **Dex** 11, **Con** 12, **Int** 1, **Wis** 9, **Cha** 8

Base Atk +0; **CMB** –3; **CMD** 7

Feats Weapon Finesse

Skills Climb +6, Perception +3

The koala's cute appearance belies the tree-climbing marsupial's aggressive nature. Koalas subsist solely on the leaves of the eucalyptus tree, which are all but inedible to most other mammals. Because of their highly selective diet, most koalas see little reason to stray from eucalyptus trees at all, and so spend most of their lives hanging onto branches or moving from crook to crook by swinging between boughs. When a koala walks (usually just to get from tree to tree), it does so on all fours.

A koala measures about 2-1/2 feet from tail to nose and can weigh up to 30 pounds.

Peacock

This bird's royal blue body is upstaged only by the magnificent array of feathers that radiate from its back.

PEACOCK	CR 1/4	

XP 100

N Small animal

Init +1; **Senses** low-light vision; Perception –2

DEFENSE

AC 12, touch 12, flat-footed 11 (+1 Dex, +1 size)

hp 4 (1d8)

Fort +2, **Ref** +3, **Will** –2

OFFENSE

Speed 20 ft., fly 40 ft. (clumsy); drift

Melee 2 talons +2 (1d3–2)

STATISTICS

Str 7, **Dex** 12, **Con** 10, **Int** 1, **Wis** 6, **Cha** 13

Base Atk +0; **CMB** –3; **CMD** 8

Feats Weapon Finesse

Skills Fly –1

SPECIAL ABILITIES

Drift (Ex) A peacock flies in short bursts, and can't use its fly speed to hover. When it flies, a peacock must end its move action by landing or perching on a solid surface.

Peacocks are the male variety of a family of pheasants collectively called peafowls. Their female counterparts, peahens, don't possess the brightly colored iridescent plumage typically associated with peacocks, and instead sport gray or brown feathers. Some cultures also breed peafowls with white plumage that may or may not have coloration on the rest of their bodies.

A peacock displays its brightly colored feathers to impress and court peahens as well as to scare off potential predators. The colorful "eye" patterns in the feathers also make them popular symbols and decorations among fortune-tellers and royalty.

While the male variety is more commonly recognized, all peafowl have identical statistics. A peacock is 3-1/2 feet tall and weighs about 10 pounds.

Penguin

This three-foot-tall, thickset bird has smooth black and white plumage that yellows around the neck, a long beak, and black flippers that lie flat against the animal's sides.

PENGUIN	CR 1/3	

XP 135

N Small animal

Init –1; **Senses** low-light vision; Perception +8

DEFENSE

AC 11, touch 10, flat-footed 11 (–1 Dex, +1 natural, +1 size)

hp 5 (1d8+1)

Fort +3, **Ref** +1, **Will** +1

OFFENSE

Speed 10 ft., swim 40 ft., toboggan 30 ft.

Melee bite +0 (1d3–1)

STATISTICS

Str 9, **Dex** 8, **Con** 13, **Int** 2, **Wis** 12, **Cha** 7

Base Atk +0; **CMB** –2; **CMD** 7

Feats Skill Focus (Perception)

Skills Perception +8, Swim +7

SQ hold breath

SPECIAL ABILITIES

Hold Breath (Ex) A penguin can hold its breath for a number of minutes equal to 6 times its Constitution score before it risks drowning.

Toboggan (Ex) On snow- or ice-covered terrain, a penguin can move at a rate of 30 feet by sliding on its belly rather than walking.

Many varieties of penguins exist, though most display similar characteristics. The penguin's most distinctive trait is the tuxedo-style coloration of its feathers, which acts as camouflage while the penguin hunts for fish underwater; the black back and flippers allow the penguin to blend in with the water when viewed from above, while its white belly resembles the bright sky when seen from below water.

A penguin of the most common variety stands roughly 3 feet tall and weighs 70 pounds. Larger species of penguin can grow to heights of 4 feet and weigh as much as 100 pounds.

Wallaby

Resembling nothing so much as a large rodent that stands on its powerful hind legs, this brown mammal has a long tail and short arms that end in five-fingered paws.

WALLABY	CR 1/3	

XP 135

N Small animal

Init +2; **Senses** low-light vision, scent; Perception +3

DEFENSE

AC 13, touch 13, flat-footed 11 (+2 Dex, +1 size)

hp 4 (1d8)

Fort +2, **Ref** +4, **Will** –1

OFFENSE

Speed 40 ft.

Melee kick +2 (1d3+1)

STATISTICS

Str 12, **Dex** 14, **Con** 11, **Int** 1, **Wis** 9, **Cha** 4

Base Atk +0; **CMB** +0; **CMD** 12

Feats Skill Focus (Acrobatics)

Skills Acrobatics +5, Perception +3

Wallabies are squat mammals that hail from a distant land far from the Inner Sea. The wallaby is often mistakenly identified as a small kangaroo. Like all marsupials, wallabies carry their newborn young in pouches at the front of their bodies. The wallaby defends itself using its strong hind legs, which it can launch quickly from under its body to deliver a powerful kick that sends would-be predators reeling. A wallaby stands about 2 feet tall and weighs 20–40 pounds.

⬥—New Improved Familiars—➤

The following new creatures can serve as familiars for characters with the Improved Familiar feat: the wily cat sith, the noble caypup, and the cryptic pseudosphinx.

Cat Sith

This slinky black feline has a single white spot on its chest. Its mannerisms and movements are eerily human.

CAT SITH	CR 2	

XP 600

CN Tiny magical beast

Init +3; **Senses** darkvision 60 ft., low-light vision, *see invisibility*; Perception +6

DEFENSE

AC 15, touch 15, flat-footed 12 (+3 Dex, +2 size)

hp 19 (3d10+3)

Fort +4, **Ref** +6, **Will** +2

OFFENSE

Speed 30 ft.

Melee 2 claws +4 (1d2−1 plus no luck), bite +4 (1d3−1)

Space 2-1/2 ft.; **Reach** 0 ft.

Special Attacks false curse (DC 15)

Spell-Like Abilities (CL 3rd; concentration +5)

Constant—*see invisibility*

3/day—*ghost sound, hypnotism, magic aura*

1/week—*rest eternal*APG

STATISTICS

Str 8, **Dex** 16, **Con** 12, **Int** 11, **Wis** 13, **Cha** 15

Base Atk +3; **CMB** +4; **CMD** 13

Feats Ability Focus (false curse), Stealthy

Skills Bluff +4, Escape Artist +5, Perception +6, Stealth +18

Languages Common; *speak with animals*

ECOLOGY

Environment temperate hills

Organization solitary, pair, or band (3–7)

Treasure standard

SPECIAL ABILITIES

False Curse (Su) Once per day, a cat sith can fool a creature into believing it has been cursed by the cat sith's black magic. The target must be within 60 feet and must be able to see the cat sith to be affected by the false curse (Will DC 15 negates). An affected creature takes a −4 penalty on attack rolls, saving throws, ability checks, and skill checks, as if affected by *bestow curse*. Because this effect is not a true curse, the target gains a new saving throw to end the effect at the beginning of each day. This is a language-dependent, mind-affecting effect that can be affected by *remove curse*. The save DC is Charisma-based.

No Luck (Su) A creature hit by a cat sith's claws must succeed at a DC 13 Will save or be stricken with lucklessness. For 1d4 rounds, the affected creature can't benefit from any luck bonuses. The save DC is Charisma-based.

Cat siths are inscrutable feline creatures that inhabit highlands around towns and cities. They resemble common housecats at a glance, but cat siths are supernatural beings that have the cunning of civilized races and strange magical powers rivaling those of fey. They're capable of easily walking balanced on just their hind legs and wearing magic boots. They can carry one object in their front paws when walking bipedally, though they can't manipulate such objects with the fine control required to use weapons, wands, and similar objects.

Unpredictable yet sophisticated, these strange beings use their unassuming appearances to infiltrate civilized areas, either serving as spies for powerful spellcasters or entertaining their own unknowable agendas.

Many cultures fear cat siths and tell myths about their otherworldly powers. Some say that letting a cat sith near an unburied corpse may allow the beast to steal the departed's soul before it has made it to the Great Beyond.

A 7th-level spellcaster with the Improved Familiar feat can gain a cat sith as a familiar. Cat siths are heavier than most housecats, weighing between 25 and 30 pounds. A cat sith is nearly 2 feet long from its nose to the base of its tail.

Caypup

This large, regal canine looks like a juvenile mastiff. It has red fur and vibrant blue eyes.

CAYPUP	CR 2	

XP 600

CG Small outsider (native)

Init +4; **Senses** darkvision 60 ft., scent; Perception +5

DEFENSE

AC 14, touch 11, flat-footed 14 (+3 natural, +1 size)

hp 22 (3d10+6)

Fort +3, **Ref** +3, **Will** +2

DR 5/cold iron

OFFENSE

Speed 30 ft.

Melee bite +6 (1d4+3)

Special Attacks thunderous growl

Spell-Like Abilities (CL 3rd; concentration +4)

   3/day—*knock, open/close, stabilize*

   1/day—*dimension door* (self plus 5 lbs. of objects only)

STATISTICS

Str 15, **Dex** 11, **Con** 14, **Int** 6, **Wis** 9, **Cha** 12

Base Atk +3; **CMB** +4; **CMD** 14

Feats Dimensional Agility^UC, Improved Initiative

Skills Acrobatics +6, Intimidate +7, Perception +5, Sense Motive +5

Languages Celestial (can't speak)

ECOLOGY

Environment any land

Organization solitary or pack (2–4)

Treasure none

SPECIAL ABILITIES

Thunderous Growl (Su) Three times per day, a caypup can issue a rumbling growl from its throat that sounds like distant thunder and scares away potential attackers. Creatures within 15 feet of the caypup must succeed at a DC 12 Will save to attack the caypup (as if affected by *sanctuary*). The caypup can choose to bestow the same effect on an adjacent ally as well. This effect lasts for 3 rounds or until the caypup or its ally attacks (whichever comes first), after which time the caypup must wait at least 1d6 rounds before using this ability again. The save DC is Charisma-based.

Cayhounds—as fickle and determined as their patron god and master, Cayden Cailean—sometimes birth pups on the Material Plane or Elysium. These half-celestial offspring are known to mortals as caypups.

Like their otherworldly forebears, caypups are driven to perform acts of good and to halt wrongdoing in the lands they roam. Caypups sometimes join adventurers in hopes of reenacting the legendary deeds of Cayden Cailean and his hound, Thunder. A 7th-level spellcaster with the Improved Familiar feat can gain a caypup as a familiar.

After maturing through infancy, caypups reach an adolescent state that they occupy for their entire lives. Resembling juvenile mastiffs with rust-red fur and piercing blue eyes, caypups are 4 feet from nose to tail and weigh about 75 pounds.

Pseudosphinx

This small creature has the body of a housecat, the wings of a falcon, and the head of a monkey.

PSEUDOSPHINX	CR 2	

XP 600

N Tiny magical beast

Init +2; **Senses** darkvision 60 ft., low-light vision; Perception +11

DEFENSE

AC 15, touch 14, flat-footed 13 (+2 Dex, +1 natural, +2 size)

hp 16 (3d10)

Fort +3, **Ref** +5, **Will** +6

DR 5/magic; **SR** 13

OFFENSE

Speed 20 ft., fly 30 ft. (average)

Melee bite +2 (1d3–3), 2 claws +2 (1d2–3)

Space 2-1/2 ft.; **Reach** 0 ft.

Special Attacks aided insight

Spell-Like Abilities (CL 5th; concentration +6)

   Constant—*comprehend languages*

   At will—*detect magic, detect secret doors*

   3/day—*burning hands, cause fear, identify, vanish*

STATISTICS

Str 5, **Dex** 14, **Con** 11, **Int** 9, **Wis** 16, **Cha** 12

Base Atk +3; **CMB** +3; **CMD** 10

Feats Alertness, Iron Will

Skills Fly +6, Perception +11, Sense Motive +5

Languages Common, Sphinx

ECOLOGY

Environment warm deserts

Organization solitary

Treasure standard

SPECIAL ABILITIES

Aided Insight (Su) Once per day, a pseudosphinx can tap into the wisdom of its ancestors to answer a question for another creature. To do so, the pseudosphinx attempts a Wisdom check, gaining a bonus on the check equal to the querent's level and treating the result of the check as the result of an appropriate Knowledge check. The pseudosphinx must be touching the querent to use this ability.

Pseudosphinxes are cat-sized, fairylike creatures thought to be distant cousins to the larger and better-known true sphinxes. They most resemble gynosphinxes, though the pseudosphinxes' monkeylike heads and tiny bodies ensure that the two species are never confused for each other. A typical pseudosphinx is 2 feet long and weighs 10 pounds.

Pseudosphinxes are rarely found in groups, and scholars are unsure whether to attribute their cryptic origins to elusive demeanors or amnesic memories. Whether they're the misbegotten progeny of generations of lesser sphinxes or the result of some magical experiment in the same deserts where sphinxes are found, none can say.

A pseudosphinx can serve as the familiar for a 7th-level spellcaster with the Improved Familiar feat.

New Unusual Familiars

While some spellcasters prefer common familiars such as birds, cats, and foxes, others seek to indulge quirkier bents by keeping magical pets. Each of the following familiars is an exotic non-animal creature that can be taken as a familiar. The special abilities these familiars grant to their masters can be found on the inside front cover of this book.

Ioun Wyrd

This creature is made of dozens of continually shifting shiny rocks and gemstones. Its centermost stone is larger than the others and occasionally pulses with dim light.

IOUN WYRD	CR 1/3

XP 135

N Tiny construct

Init +2; **Senses** blindsight 30 ft.; Perception +2

DEFENSE

AC 15, touch 15, flat-footed 12 (+2 Dex, +1 dodge, +2 size)

hp 5 (1d10)

Fort +0, **Ref** +2, **Will** +2

Immune construct traits

OFFENSE

Speed fly 30 ft. (average)

Melee slam +0 (1d4–3)

Space 2-1/2 ft.; **Reach** 0 ft.

STATISTICS

Str 4, **Dex** 15, **Con** —, **Int** 3, **Wis** 14, **Cha** 5

Base Atk +1; **CMB** +1; **CMD** 9

Feats Dodge

Skills Fly +10, Perception +2

Languages Common (can't speak)

SQ ioun affinity, share iouns

ECOLOGY

Environment any

Organization solitary

Treasure none or 1d4–1 random *ioun stones*

SPECIAL ABILITIES

Ioun Affinity (Su) An ioun wyrd may integrate a number of *ioun stones* into its body up to 1 + 1/2 its Hit Dice. Because an ioun wyrd sees all *ioun stones* as equal and gains no benefits from them, the wyrd's *ioun stones* can be swapped out by any creature the wyrd trusts.

Share Iouns (Su) A character with an ioun wyrd familiar gains the benefits of its *ioun stones* as long as he's within 30 feet of the ioun wyrd.

Ioun wyrds appear to be extraplanar creatures somewhat resembling earth elementals, but they're actually bizarre constructs, assembled in laboratories throughout Golarion to serve equally unusual masters. Ioun wyrds have occasionally been found in the wild, typically in regions near hidden wizards' towers or discreet arcane laboratories in the Nexian highlands or Thuvian deserts, if only because mages sometimes find it difficult to keep track of these wily beings. Left to their own devices, ioun wyrds seek out abandoned mines, gem-rich caverns, or lonely grottos where they might find pretty stones, which they see as somehow related to themselves.

A typical ioun wyrd is roughly 2 feet in diameter and weighs 15–20 pounds.

Construction

An ioun wyrd is made of small gemstones, lodestones, and bits of granite which are coated with 500 gp worth of alchemical materials. A single functional *ioun stone* must also be present, which the ioun wyrd takes as the first *ioun stone* to be integrated into its body with its ioun affinity.

IOUN WYRD

CL 5th; **Price** 1,500 gp plus *ioun stone*

CONSTRUCTION

Requirements Craft Construct, *animate object*, *lesser geas*; **Skill** Knowledge (arcana) DC 15; **Cost** 1,000 gp plus *ioun stone*

Leopard Slug

This dark yellow, hand-length slug is covered in a pattern of black spots and stripes.

LEOPARD SLUG	CR 1/8

XP 50

N Diminutive vermin

Init –3; **Senses** darkvision 30 ft.; Perception –2

DEFENSE

AC 11, touch 11, flat-footed 11 (–3 Dex, +4 size)

hp 5 (1d8+1)

Fort +3, **Ref** –3, **Will** –2

Immune mind-affecting effects

OFFENSE

Speed 10 ft., climb 10 ft.

Space 1 ft.; **Reach** 0 ft.

STATISTICS

Str 1, **Dex** 4, **Con** 12, **Int** —, **Wis** 7, **Cha** 9

Base Atk +0; **CMB** –7; **CMD** –2

Skills Climb +3

SQ compression, slime strand, suction

ECOLOGY

Environment temperate forests
Organization solitary, pair, or cornucopia (3–10)
Treasure none

SPECIAL ABILITIES

Slime Strand (Ex) A leopard slug can turn its mucus into a 30-foot-long strand, much like a spider's silk. It can hang from this strand indefinitely, and lower itself safely at a rate of 10 feet per round. It can climb back up the strand at the same rate. Once the slug breaks contact with the strand, the mucus disintegrates in 1d4 rounds.

Suction (Ex) A leopard slug secretes sticky mucus, which allows it to apply its 10-foot climb speed to any surface, even sheer walls and ceilings. Once attached to a surface, it has no chance of falling off, unless it's grappled and actively peeled away.

Leopard slugs are among the largest species of slug, and are certainly the most distinctive due to their unique coloration, which often resembles that of a leopard. This characteristic pattern allows leopard slugs to blend in with foliage and stones in the forest environments they call home. Occasionally, one can find more colorful varieties of leopard slug (such as fluorescent orange, bright yellow, or flaming red), bred specifically as pets or familiars by the esoteric masters who prefer such creatures.

Leopard slugs are about 6 inches long and weigh less than a pound.

Petrifern

This tiny, unassuming tree is shaped like a miniature person, with branches for arms and roots for feet.

PETRIFERN	CR 1/6

XP 65
N Diminutive plant
Init –1; **Senses** blindsight 30 ft.; Perception –2

DEFENSE

AC 15, touch 13, flat-footed 15 (–1 Dex, +2 natural, +4 size)
hp 5 (1d8+1)
Fort +3, **Ref** –1, **Will** –2
Defensive Abilities toxic secretion; **Immune** plant traits

OFFENSE

Speed 20 ft.
Space 1 ft.; **Reach** 0 ft.

STATISTICS

Str 2, **Dex** 9, **Con** 13, **Int** —, **Wis** 6, **Cha** 9
Base Atk +0; **CMB** –5; **CMD** 1
SQ petrify

ECOLOGY

Environment any forests
Organization solitary, bundle (2–14), or hive (15–60)
Treasure none

SPECIAL ABILITIES

Petrify (Ex) A petrifern can petrify itself as a standard action in order to defend itself from predators. When it does so,

While most familiars are Tiny animals or magical beasts, spellcasters may acquire larger or more unusual creatures during their travels, which impart certain rules effects that should be considered at the table.

Small familiars threaten the areas around them like other Small creatures, and can be used to flank enemies—though both familiars and their masters are generally loath to employ such tactics, as the result is often a dead familiar. Small familiars are also harder to keep on a master's person than Tiny or smaller familiars; some form of magic item, like a *bag of holding*, is usually required.

Construct, plant, and vermin familiars gain an Intelligence score, and they lose the mindless trait if they had it. If such familiars lack a language, they communicate with their masters and other creatures of their kind (greensting scorpions with other scorpions, mobile plant creatures with other mobile plant creatures, and so on) by way of a strange combination of behaviors, slight changes in coloration, and sometimes even the excretion of scents or pheromones. Other types of creatures can't understand this communication without magical aid.

Outsiders and undead creatures are normally available only with the Improved Familiar feat, and require no other special rules.

the petrifern's natural armor bonus to AC increases by 5, it gains resistance 10 to cold and fire, and it can take 20 on Stealth checks to appear as a sprout or fallen tree branch. While petrified, the petrifern can't move or take any actions. A petrifern can remain petrified indefinitely, and can cease its petrification as a standard action.

Toxic Secretion (Ex) Petriferns secrete a bitter toxin meant to make them distasteful to predators. Once per day when a creature touches a petrifern, the plant can release its toxin, causing the attacker to become sickened for 1d4 rounds if it fails a DC 11 Fortitude saving throw. The save DC is Constitution-based.

The petrifern is an unusual plant creature that resembles a small humanoid-shaped fern, and is able to walk about on its roots. It has the unusual ability to petrify itself at will, hardening its branches and leaves to resemble those of a plant that has been fossilized by natural means. A petrifern's chemical makeup not only allows it to petrify itself, but also doubles as a toxin that the plant can emit from its foliage when it senses danger.

Like all plants, petriferns subsist on sunlight, oxygen, and water. But unlike most flora, they can relocate themselves to ensure they always receive an abundance of nutrients. Once rooted, a petrifern typically petrifies itself until either the nearby soil is depleted of nutrients or external factors cause it to seek sustenance elsewhere.

Petriferns reach a maximum height of 1 foot and weigh up to 3 pounds.

Next Month!

Tired of seeing adventure only from a distance? Dive straight into the heart of combat with *Player Companion: Melee Tactics Toolbox*! Featuring tons of never-before-seen rules options, this volume covers advice for up-close combat—ranging from one-on-one duels to unexpected brawls. Included are new feats, melee weapons, and magic items to give you all the tools and techniques you need to go toe to toe with Golarion's most dangerous foes. Whether you're guarding your party's spellcaster from hordes of goblins or wrestling fleeing criminals to the ground, the *Melee Tactics Toolbox* is your go-to source for tips, tactics, and much more!

Would You Like to Know More?

You've invested in feats to bolster your familiar, taken an archetype to tie it more closely to your character concept, and learned spells to keep your familiar safe in combat. But getting the most out of your familiar requires more than just a pouch to carry its extra rations. The following Pathfinder accessories offer a wide range of gear and options for your familiar!

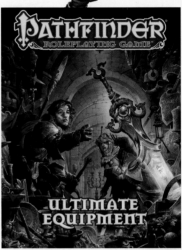

Familiars aren't the only animal allies an adventurer can pick up. Find yourself a companion or pet with new rules and options for various classes in *Pathfinder Player Companion: Animal Archive*.

When it comes to familiars, there's a whole menagerie to choose from. Get the full statistics for some of the most popular familiar choices—including the goat, otter, and pig—in *Pathfinder RPG Bestiary 3*.

Want to buy a cage to carry your archaeopteryx around in while you're exploring a city? Need a hawking glove for your familiar to land on? You can find this gear and more in *Pathfinder RPG Ultimate Equipment*.